THE GLORIOUS YEARS OF THE SOUTHERN RAILWAY

PETER TUFFREY

GREAT NORTHERN

ACKNOWLEDGEMENTS

I would like to thank the following people for their help: Roger Arnold, David Burrill, John Chalcraft, Paul Chancellor, Peter Crangle, David Dippie, John Law, Hugh Parkin, Bill Reed, David P. Williams.

Special thanks are due to my son, Tristram Tuffrey for his help and encouragement throughout the course of this project.

Unless otherwise stated, all pictures are from the author's collection.

In the latter years of the SR, colour photography had only just begun and was an expensive activity that very few photographers could afford. Consequently, few photographs of SR subjects are known to have survived, and the quality of these in many cases is poor. The Author would like to express sincere thanks to David P. Williams for his skill in producing the fine colour illustrations on the front and back covers of this book. They have been painstakingly put together by digitally adding colour to original monochrome photographs, with the aim of recreating what the photographer could see in the camera viewfinder when the shutter was released.

Front Cover: Bulleid 'West Country' Class Pacific no. 21C101 *Exeter* hauls the 'Devon Belle' up the formidable 1 in 36 of Mortehoe bank on the climb out of Ilfracombe with the London-bound service.

Cover: *Top* – All West of England trains to and from Waterloo stopped and changed engines at Salisbury in SR and early BR days. In this photograph, Maunsell's rebuild of 'Urie Arthur' no. 747 *Elaine* has just been attached to this train from Waterloo at Platform 3, which it will take as far as Exeter. There, the train would be split, with the front coaches going to Plymouth and the rear portion heading for North Devon and Cornwall (with fresh motive power).

Middle left – D1 Class no. 2252 entered service as no. 252 *Buckhurst* in 1882. The locomotive went on to be one of the last class members in service when condemned during 1950. No. 2252 is seen at an unidentified location before Nationalisation.

Middle right – The first SR 'Schools' Class 4-4-0, no. 900 *Eton* is at Cannon Street in the mid-1930s on a Hastings train. Alongside, 'King Arthur' Class no. 800 *Sir Meleaus de Lile* heads a Ramsgate express.

Bottom – The LSWR's ninety A12 'Jubilee' 0-4-2s of 1887 were that Company's equivalent to the 'Gladstone' 0-4-2s of the LB&SCR, being built at the same time and carrying out the same kind of duty. Seen in clean condition at Nine Elms on Saturday, 29th May 1937, A12 no. 617 carries a later Drummond boiler. To the right of the locomotive is ex-Kent & East Sussex 0-8-0T no. 949 *Hecate*.

Great Northern Books Limited
PO Box 1380, Bradford, BD5 5FB
www.greatnorthernbooks.co.uk

ISBN: 978-1-914227-85-1

Design and layout: David Burrill

CIP Data
A catalogue for this book is available from the British Library

CONTENTS

INTRODUCTION

Whilst the Southern Railway was the smallest of the 'Big Four' railway companies created by the Railways Act 1921, none of the others dealt with the traffic tribulations as tenaciously over the inter-war period. In doing so, the SR created the largest electric system in the world at the time and remained relatively profitable, whereas the other three companies were hampered by their reliance on freight traffic.

Over 100 railway companies were affected by the Grouping of 1923 which was the result of the First World War. When hostilities broke out, the British railway system was taken over for the duration by the Government and operated under the Railway Executive Committee. The cohesion this achieved raised questions as to the fate of the railway companies when peace returned. Nationalisation had been mooted as early as the 1840s and this action was again raised. Sir Eric Geddes, who was made Minister of Transport in 1919, presented a white paper on the future of the railways. He was opposed to Nationalisation but saw the original arrangements as undesirable so recommended forming larger companies from the existing concerns. Despite protests from railway interests, the Railways Act of 1921 was passed and scheduled to go into force on 1st January 1923.

On this date, the Southern Railway began operating. The new company's territory ran from south of the River Thames to the Channel ports, with a branch into the West Country. The area served was taken from three main railway companies: the London & South Western Railway; London, Brighton & South Coast Railway; South Eastern & Chatham Railway. Several smaller companies absorbed included those working on the Isle of Wight. The largest company of the group was the LSWR. Formed from the London & Southampton Railway, the LSWR was particularly ambitious and early on targeted South West England, in addition to developing main line and suburban services. By the turn of the century, the company was important for traffic to Exeter, North Devon and North Cornwall. Though initially involved with the docks at Southampton, the LSWR purchased the operating company in the 1890s and further developed the facilities there. The SR also made improvements and during the company's existence, the port handled around half of the passengers leaving England, in addition to dealing with nearly 20 million tons of goods. Military traffic was also important to areas served by the LSWR, particularly during times of armed conflict, such as the Boer War or World War One.

The South Eastern & Chatham Railway was the result of a merger between the competing London, Chatham & Dover Railway and South Eastern Railway on 1st January 1899. The latter company was established first and using existing lines to London, extended eastward to Tonbridge, Ashford, Folkestone, Dover, Ramsgate and Margate throughout the 1840s. The SER made an inroad westward during the 1850s by reaching Guildford and Reading. In the 1860s, the company improved the main line by diverting northward at Tonbridge to reduce journey times. As the SER built their railway through the middle of Kent, people in the north were determined to be included in the network. The East Kent Railway was formed in the early 1850s and built a line from Strood to Faversham which opened during 1858, then extended to Canterbury and Dover in 1862. At the same time, the company, now known as the London, Chatham & Dover Railway, was working into London, first to Victoria, then in the mid-1860s, Farringdon Street.

With this rapid advance, the LC&DR found itself over-extended financially and in the late 1860s, the company was bankrupt. Yet, with strong management, the LC&DR recovered and proved a formidable rival to the SER. By the 1890s, the competition was too much and the pair entered into an agreement to unite and from 1st January 1899 both operated under a Joint Committee as the South Eastern & Chatham Railway. Up to the Grouping, this allowed some general improvements to be made to services and rolling stock.

A pioneering railway was the Surrey Iron Railway which ran from Wandsworth to Croydon and opened in 1806. Operating as a plateway, the success of railways in the North of England led the SIR to convert to an edgeway using the course of the defunct Croydon Canal. Opening in 1839, this became the gateway to London for several companies. One was the London & Brighton Railway which started construction from the London & Croydon Railway in 1838 and opened in stages from mid-July to mid-September 1841. Five years later, the L&CR and L&BR merged together, incorporating some lines under construction as well, to form the London, Brighton & South Coast Railway. The new company's territory soon expanded to reach Portsmouth, Newhaven, Eastbourne and St Leonards. Unlike the other constituent companies, the LB&SCR held a dominant position in the surrounding area and had amicable relations with bordering railways. This allowed a focus on services for the main line and an extensive suburban network. The latter faced competition from early tramways in the late 19th and early 20th centuries and the LB&SCR was an early adopter of electric trains, though favoured an overhead system.

The Southern Railway came into being on 1st January 1923 and several years passed where the company rationalised and improved the new system. Overseeing the task was Sir Herbert Walker, who took the position of General Manager in 1924. As the head of the LSWR, he had pioneered the introduction of electric services using the third rail system and continued this scheme with the SR whilst keeping a keen eye on the financial position of the company and economising where necessary.

The SR was primarily a passenger railway and in the mid-1920s this amounted to around 17 million journeys or 70% of the total traffic. This was 27% higher than the Great Western Railway, which had a 43% to 56% division of passenger journeys to freight tons moved. The London Midland & Scottish Railway and London & North Eastern Railway both had around a 40% to 60% split which would go on to hurt the companies when trade conditions worsened in the late 1920s and early 1930s. The SR's large passenger share clearly defined where investment was necessary and this would deliver later when the named expresses and regularly scheduled electric services came into operation.

Richard Maunsell was made Chief Mechanical Engineer of the SR and he was given the task of overseeing the 2,281 locomotives inherited from the constituents, as well as nearly 7,500 carriages, over 36,000 wagons and around 460 electric vehicles. He also had the responsibility of producing new rolling stock to meet the needs of the new network. Previously employed by the SE&CR, he had first-hand knowledge of bringing together the stock of different companies and integrating new designs to meet broad requirements. To meet initial needs, some existing designs were perpetuated, such as Robert Urie's H15, N15 and S15 Class 4-6-0s. Though struggling in their initial specifications, once modified by Maunsell the engines performed to expectations. Maunsell's 'statement' design was the 'Lord Nelson' Class 4-6-0 for Dover and Folkestone boat trains and the locomotives, for a time, were the most powerful of the type in Britain. Similarly, the V Class, known as the 'Schools' Class, held the title for the 4-4-0 wheel arrangement. These locomotives were used on intermediate trains to Dover, Ramsgate, Hastings, Portsmouth, etc. Amongst his other designs were the U Class 2-6-0, W Class 2-6-4T and Q Class 0-6-0.

Retiring in 1937, Maunsell was succeeded by O.V.S. Bulleid who had been Sir Nigel Gresley's Personal Assistant on the Great Northern Railway and LNER. With a flair for innovation, Bulleid was unrestricted with his ideas and though having some flaws, his Pacifics had a firm foundation to serve the SR and Southern Region for many years. Maunsell had been restricted with his plans for locomotives owing to the electrification schemes of the 1920s and 1930s, yet with war looming, the SR Board authorised new locomotives for expresses and medium traffic in the late 1930s. Despite wartime restrictions, Bulleid produced the 'Merchant Navy' Class Pacific in 1941 and the slightly smaller 'West Country' and 'Battle of Britain' Pacifics from 1945. Both types of Pacifics had an 'air smoothed' casing creating a distinct identity of the classes, whilst another Bulleid design, the Q1 0-6-0, had a unique appearance. This was necessary to save as much weight as possible and create an unhindered environment for enginemen to service components.

Electrification was a priority for the pre-Grouping companies and the SR also embraced the system. This was driven by rising passenger numbers and low line capacity in the approaches to the London stations. Increasing the number of tracks was impractical and more steam services would have created greater congestion owing to slower acceleration times of locomotives. Development of electric technology during the First World War also increased the cost effectiveness of electric transport, as well as electric trains being easier, simpler, and required fewer staff to operate.

In 1924, plans were announced for the electrification of the ex-SE&CR lines, as well as extensions to routes already started by the LSWR. At the same time, rationalisations and rebuilding works were carried out at stations, as well as new facilities provided as suburban London expanded. During 1925, the first SR electric services were offered every 20 minutes and on the Waterloo to Guildford line, trains ran between the two places some 20 minutes quicker than with steam. In the same year, the first SE&CR route electric trains began after much work to improve the infrastructure. Part of this saw the installation of four-aspect colour light signalling which was the world's first instance of use. As the suburban lines became electrified in the late 1920s, Sir Herbert Walker announced plans to convert the route to Brighton and this was achieved in just two years as around 150 miles of track were dealt with. The new services were popular and increased revenue and passenger numbers. Further schemes were put forward in the early 1930s and this was helped by the financial climate of the period. To encourage trade and employment, the Government offered very attractive loan rates to the 'Big Four' railways and the SR took advantage by taking £6 million of the funds for electrification and other improvements. By the end of the 1930s, the SR had 1,759 miles of lines electrified. Of around 84 million miles travelled by services, almost half had been done by electric trains, whilst significant savings had been made in many areas compared to steam.

Further progress was halted by the outbreak of the Second World War. Like the other railway companies, the SR was active in assisting the war effort in many ways. Initially, this was the evacuation of children from areas like London, then transporting the British Expeditionary Force to points of embarkation on the South Coast. The SR was subsequently instrumental in returning the personnel as part of the Dunkirk evacuation and dispersing troops to places across the country. The SR was also in the front line of attacks by the German air force but the company and staff were able to deal with damage quickly and efficiently to keep the railway moving. The SR's workshops were involved with war production, such as guns, gliders and landing craft. Brighton Works, which had been rundown, was brought back into service and built a number of locomotives for the SR, the Railway Executive Committee, as well as the LNER.

The war had left the railways of Britain battered and also changed the political opinion of the general public. A Labour Government swept to power in the general election of 1945 under policies of widespread Nationalisation. The will was now there for the railways to fall under Government control as part of the Transport Act 1947. This created the British Transport Commission, which in turn oversaw British Railways. The new regions were organised on similar lines to the 'Big Four' and the Southern Region was to operate former Southern Railway lines from 1st January 1948.

Whilst there might have been cautious optimism in 1923, there was less as 1948 approached. People, perhaps correctly, guessed that the public ownership of the railway and the bureaucracy involved in such an enterprise would not operate the railways as successfully as the SR did during the inter-war period. This was truly a golden age for the company as many elements came together to create an exciting and prosperous time.

CONSTITUENTS

Above LYNTON & BARNSTAPLE RAILWAY
Manning Wardle 2-6-2T locomotive *Exe* has a train at Lynton in the early 20th century. Photograph from Rail Archive Stephenson courtesy Rail-Online.

Below LYNTON & BARNSTAPLE RAILWAY
Following the First World War, traffic on the Lynton & Barnstaple Railway went into terminal decline. Despite efforts by the Southern Railway to improve fortunes, the company was forced to close the line from 29th September 1935. Baldwin Locomotive Works 2-4-2T engine *Lyn* is seen at Woody Bay station with a train for Lynton at the time of Grouping. Photograph by Reginald S. Clark from Rail Archive Stephenson courtesy Rail-Online.

Above LONDON, BRIGHTON & SOUTH COAST RAILWAY
William Stroudley's B1 Class 0-4-2 design won a gold medal at the Paris Exhibition in 1889. The engines were used on main line expresses until the turn of the century when superseded. Twenty-six locomotives survived to SR ownership. No. 197, originally named *Jonas Levy*, passes Tooting Common with a passenger train in the early 20th century.

Below LONDON, BRIGHTON & SOUTH COAST RAILWAY
Stroudley B1 Class 0-4-2 locomotive no. 187, originally named *Philip Rose*, stands at Brighton station during the early 20th century. Photograph from Rail Archive Stephenson courtesy Rail-Online.

Above LONDON, CHATHAM & DOVER RAILWAY

With suburban traffic expanding in the mid-1860s, the London, Chatham & Dover Railway was obliged to provide new rolling stock for services. William Martley was advised to use an 0-4-2WT design based on engines in service for the Great Northern Railway. No. 547 was amongst this group of 14 'Scotchmen' Class locomotives. Seen at Victoria station in the early 20th century, no. 547 was condemned during 1909. Photograph from Rail Archive Stephenson courtesy Rail-Online.

Below LONDON, CHATHAM & DOVER RAILWAY

Built in June 1863, Martley 'Bluebell' Class, later P Class, 2-4-0 *Hyacinth* poses for an early photograph in the late 1860s. Photograph from Rail Archive Stephenson courtesy Rail-Online.

Above LONDON & SOUTH WESTERN RAILWAY

Adams O2 Class 0-4-4T no. 227 is at Lyme Regis station in the early 20th century. A short branch of around six miles opened from Axminster in 1903 and was in use to late November 1965. No. 227 was built at Nine Elms Works during November 1894 and ran to June 1933 when amongst the first class withdrawals.

Below LONDON & SOUTH WESTERN RAILWAY

By the late 1840s, the LSWR and LB&SCR were running services to Portsmouth. During the 1870s, the companies agreed to work together on a branch to Portsmouth Harbour and this opened on 2nd October 1876. LSWR Drummond C8 Class 4-4-0 no. 292 stands on the left at Portsmouth Harbour station in 1903, whilst LB&SCR Stroudley B1 Class 0-4-2 no. 219 *Cleveland* is right with a train for Brighton. Photograph by H.F. Hall from Rail Archive Stephenson courtesy Rail-Online.

Above SOUTH EASTERN & CHATHAM RAILWAY
James Stirling joined the South Eastern Railway in 1878 and was met with a need for a suitable suburban locomotive. In his previous position with the Glasgow & South Western Railway, an 0-4-4T had been produced and formed the basis of the Q Class introduced during 1881. Production lasted to 1897 when 118 locomotives had entered service. One of this number has been caught approaching Martin Mill station – north of Dover – during the early 20th century. Photograph from Rail Archive Stephenson courtesy Rail-Online.

Below SOUTH EASTERN & CHATHAM RAILWAY
James Cudworth was inspired by a batch of E.B. Wilson 2-4-0s recently purchased by the South Eastern Railway to perpetuate the design for a mixed traffic locomotive. Known as the 118 Class, 110 locomotives to the general design were constructed by several manufacturers from 1858 to 1874. The last batch was delivered from Dübs & Co. and this engine, no. 247A, was amongst the group. Nearly all were reboilered over the years and had a service life of around 30 years. No. 247A, which is at Selsdon Road station in the early 20th century, was condemned during October 1905. Photograph from Rail Archive Stephenson courtesy Rail-Online.

PASSENGER LOCOMOTIVES

Above ADAMS T3 CLASS 4-4-0 – NO. 569

In the late 19th century, William Adams produced the T3 Class 4-4-0 design for use on the line to Exeter. Finding success there to Grouping, the formation of the SR and the rise of new types, as well as electrification, saw the T3s become surplus to requirements. Built for the LSWR in June 1893, no. 569 was amongst the early withdrawals in January 1932. The locomotive is pictured during the mid- to late 1920s.

Below STROUDLEY B1 CLASS 0-4-2 – NO. 172

The LB&SCR built 36 B1, or 'Gladstone', Class 0-4-2 locomotives for express services from 1882 and 1891. But for William Stroudley's untimely death in the latter year, further examples were planned. His successor turned to the 4-4-0 arrangement for new engines of the type. No. 172, originally named *Littlehampton*, was the last B1 completed during April 1891 and was condemned in September 1933. The engine is at New Cross shed in October 1929. Photograph courtesy Colour-Rail.

760
SE&CR

Above **WAINWRIGHT L CLASS 4-4-0 – NO. 770**

As with the other 'Big Four' railway companies after Grouping, the Southern experienced the problem of duplicated running numbers. This was partially solved initially by adding a prefix letter to denote the parent company. In the case of SE&CR locomotives, this was an 'A', representing Ashford Works. Wainwright L Class 4-4-0 no. 770 has the prefix above the number on the tender, yet still retains the SE&CR company plate on the cab side. The locomotive was eventually renumbered 1770 in the late 1920s. Photograph courtesy Rail Photoprints.

Opposite above **WAINWRIGHT L CLASS 4-4-0 – NO. 760**

When the London, Brighton & South Coast Railway merged with the South Eastern Railway, the two companies' rolling stock departments also joined together. As the heads of the LB&SCR and SER locomotive sections retired, the new company promoted SER Carriage & Wagon Superintendent Harry Wainwright. Of around half a dozen new designs he produced, the L Class 4-4-0 was the final one before his retirement in 1914. Not yet sent to the manufacturers, incoming Superintendent Richard Maunsell modified certain features, such as changing to piston valves and introducing superheating. A total of 22 was ordered, with 12 from Beyer, Peacock & Co. and the remainder delivered from Borsig, Germany. These latter engines were assembled at Ashford Works by Borsig employees just before the First World War. No. 760 was the first to be completed by Beyer, Peacock & Co. in August 1914 and the last appeared during October. The locomotive is at rest in a yard around the time of Grouping. Photograph courtesy Rail Photoprints.

Opposite below **BILLINTON B2 CLASS 4-4-0 – NO. 203**

R.J. Billinton's B2 Class 4-4-0 appeared in the mid-1890s for traffic to Portsmouth, yet initially struggled with boiler problems and rough riding. Several revisions to the design occurred, with all becoming B2X Class members before the First World War. No. 203, seen departing Victoria station, c.1925, was built in March 1897, then converted during February 1909. Withdrawal occurred in October 1930.

JOHN
28

BEACHY HEAD
SOUTHERN
424

Above WAINWRIGHT L CLASS 4-4-0 – NO. 771

The Beyer, Peacock & Co.-built Wainwright L Class 4-4-0s were fitted originally with Robinson superheaters, whilst those erected by Borsig had the Schmidt type. No. 771 was the last of the batch built in England, being completed during October 1914. The engine survived Grouping and Nationalisation, going on to be withdrawn in December 1961 and the last class member in traffic. Photograph courtesy Rail Photoprints.

Opposite above WAINWRIGHT F1 CLASS 4-4-0 – NO. 28

For South Eastern Railway express services, mainly to the ports, a new locomotive was necessary in the early 1880s. James Stirling used his experience to produce a 4-4-0 which was an asset to the company for many years subsequently. The first F Class engine, no. 205, left Ashford Works in 1883 and a further 87 appeared from there to 1898. No. 28 was the first of a batch of seven to be completed during 1889. In the early 20th century under Wainwright, many members of the F Class were part of a reboilering programme which saw the original domeless type replaced with a domed boiler working at a slightly higher pressure. Reclassified F1, the locomotives were kept employed into the 1930s, some even reaching to the late 1940s. During June 1933, no. 28 has been caught between duties at Hastings. Photograph by W. Boyden courtesy Colour-Rail.

Opposite below MARSH H2 CLASS 4-4-2 – NO. 424

D.E. Marsh was well positioned to meet the need for a suitable express locomotive for the London, Brighton & South Coast Railway. Before his appointment with the company in 1904, Marsh served as Chief Assistant Mechanical Engineer and Works Manager at Doncaster for the Great Northern Railway and H.A. Ivatt. The latter developed the famous Atlantic locomotives at the time which achieved great success on the East Coast Main Line. Marsh's H1 Atlantic was quite similar to the GNR product, with the main differences being longer piston stroke and higher working pressure, which was unusual for the time at 200 lb per sq. in. Late in his tenure, Marsh became ill and L.B. Billinton substituted for him. The decision was made to build more Atlantics, but with superheaters, though the working pressure was reduced to 170 lb per sq. in. The new engines, H2 Class, joined the H1s on the Brighton expresses and continued this role into the 1920s. H2 Class no. 424 *Beachy Head* is pictured at Bognor during September 1930. The locomotive went on to be the last H2 in service and was withdrawn during April 1958. Photograph by W. Boyden courtesy Colour-Rail.

1749
SOUTHERN

SOUTHERN
1079

Above DRUMMOND L12 CLASS 4-4-0 – NO. 418
Even though the LSWR was equipped with a number of T9 Class 4-4-0s for express duties, the Board desired a new type in the early 20th century. Drummond produced the L12 Class 4-4-0 in 1904 and 1905, with a total of 20 examples, though there was little deviation from the T9 design. No. 418 was an early example built during July 1904. The class went on to be superheated and the locomotive was equipped in October 1919. Becoming no. 30418 after Nationalisation, the engine survived to June 1951. No. 418 is pictured c. 1930 working a freight service.

Opposite above WAINWRIGHT D CLASS 4-4-0 – NO. 1749
Soon after taking the helm of the SE&CR, Wainwright produced the D Class 4-4-0 to be used on coastal expresses. Fifty-one locomotives were built over six years from 1901, including no. 1749 which was constructed at Vulcan Foundry during October 1903. Under Maunsell, a number of D Class engines were fitted with a new boiler featuring a Belpaire firebox and no. 1749 was amongst them. Seen at Stewarts Lane shed around Nationalisation, the locomotive was condemned in November 1961. Photograph by W. Boyden courtesy Colour-Rail.

Opposite below WAINWRIGHT F1 CLASS 4-4-0 – NO. 1079
Two F Class 4-4-0s were reboilered to F1 in 1903 and five followed during 1904. No. 1079 was part of the latter group and other changes made at the time included new cylinders as well as the provision of a cab. The peak year for conversions was 1906 when 13 were carried out and in total 75 F1s were created by 1916. The process was to end then, yet no. 20 was involved in a bad collision during November 1919 and from parts salvaged no. 185 became the last F1. No. 1079 would have been provided with a short smokebox when new, but from 1915 a longer one was fitted when necessary. The locomotive is at St Leonards in June 1933 and survived to August 1946. Photograph by W. Boyden courtesy Colour-Rail.

BILLINTON B4X CLASS 4-4-0 – NO. 2060
No. 2060 is leaving Barnham Junction with a Portsmouth to London Bridge train during 1938. Photograph by C.R.L. Coles from the Dave Cobbe Collection courtesy Rail Photoprints.

Above MAUNSELL L1 CLASS 4-4-0 – NO. 1758

A southbound express calls at Tonbridge station on 27th May 1939. Maunsell L1 no. 1758 is the locomotive. Photograph by George C. Lander courtesy Rail Photoprints.

Below MAUNSELL U1 CLASS 2-6-0 – NO. 1892

U1 Class no. 1892 is approaching Clapham Junction with a Victoria to Tunbridge Wells West train during June 1946. Photograph by C.R.L. Coles from the Dave Cobbe Collection courtesy Rail Photoprints.

Opposite URIE N15 CLASS 4-6-0 – NO. 787

Enginemen prepare Urie N15 Class no. 787 *Sir Menadeuke* to leave with an express from Waterloo station during the late 1920s. After Grouping, the SR desired to replace older designs and with workshop capacity stretched, turned to the North British Locomotive Company. An initial batch of 20 was ordered, followed by an increase of ten. These appeared in the summer of 1925, with no. 787 amongst this group. Photograph by B. Whicher from Rail Archive Stephenson courtesy Rail Online.

Below URIE N15 CLASS 4-6-0 – NO. 453

As a publicity exercise, the Southern Railway decided to name all express passenger engines in early 1925. New Urie N15 Class 4-6-0s were entering service at the time and the decision was made to christen the class after characters in the legend of King Arthur. No. 453 was the most recent class member to enter service and took *King Arthur*. The locomotive is pictured in the mid- to late 1920s.

387

12

Above URIE N15 CLASS 4-6-0 – NO. 783

Richard Maunsell became Chief Mechanical Engineer of the SR at Grouping and despite having his own design ideas, met the pressing needs of the running department with existing designs. Yet for the new N15s, some changes were made to modernise and improve performance. One concerned the blastpipe and chimney arrangements which reduced some steaming troubles experienced by the original LSWR locomotives. This presumably caused a problem with drifting exhaust as trials were necessary with several forms of smoke deflection devices. No. 783 *Sir Gillemere* was one of the engines to participate in these and had a cowl fitted above the smokebox to catch air that would carry the exhaust upwards and away. Along with other attempts to deflect the smoke, this was unsuccessful and after testing in a wind tunnel, the best form of deflector was slightly curved metal plates fitted to the running plate either side of the smokebox. The modification was class-wide and carried out in the late 1920s. No. 783 was later involved in a second experiment which took place under Bulleid during the Second World War. This saw three blastpipes and chimneys fitted in an effort to disperse exhaust quickly and not alert enemy aircraft. No. 783 was modified in November 1940 and has the arrangement in the above image.

Opposite URIE N15 CLASS 4-6-0 – NO. 782

No. 782 *Sir Brian* was new from the NBLC in July 1925 and is being admired at Waterloo station shortly after that date before departing with an express for South West England. The N15s built by the company were slightly different in having a loading gauge to suit areas now in the SR's territory, rather than just the LSWR's routes. Also, a new design of cab was fitted and the smokebox door was secured by several fasteners instead of the usual handles. No. 782 was in service to September 1962. Photograph by F.H. Stingemore from Rail Archive Stephenson courtesy Rail-Online.

SOUTHERN
765

Opposite URIE N15 CLASS 4-6-0 – NO. 765
Employment on the LSWR's boat trains was the original role for the Urie N15 Class 4-6-0s when introduced in 1918. The destinations included Portsmouth, Southampton and Weymouth. With the formation of the SR and introduction of new class members, the sphere of operations increased and included Dover on the ex-SE&CR. NBLC-built N15, no. 765 *Sir Gareth* is departing Dover Marine station with a boat train destined for London Victoria in the mid-1920s. The locomotive was new during May 1925 and had a service life of just over 37 years. Photograph from Rail Archive Stephenson courtesy Rail-Online.

Below URIE N15 CLASS 4-6-0 – NO. 763
No. 763 *Sir Bors de Ganis* was the first of the order from the NBLC to be completed during May 1925. The locomotive is at an unidentified location around this time as smoke deflectors are yet to be fitted and the 'E' prefix above the number is still in use. The latter feature was present to 1931 when the fleet was renumbered. No. 763 remained the same as ex-LSWR locomotives went unchanged and the other constituents' class members had a set figure added to the original number.

SOUTHERN
767

Above URIE N15 CLASS 4-6-0 – NO. 772
No. 772 *Sir Percivale* was another N15 Class member that was part of the smoke deflection trials of 1926-1927. The locomotive had long, straight deflectors fitted and secured by a bracket at the top connected to the smokebox. As mentioned, shorter curved metal plates became standard. The N15s were the first British locomotive class to be given smoke deflectors.

Opposite URIE N15 CLASS 4-6-0 – NO. 767
Headed by no. 767 *Sir Valence*, the 11.00 boat train from Victoria rushes through a busy Bromley South station during 1927. Following Grouping, the SR operated four boat trains on the ex-SE&CR between Victoria and Dover, with the other departures being 09.05, 14.00 and 16.30. The latter had the quickest time of the group, with arrival in Paris scheduled for around midnight. The 11.00 became the 'Golden Arrow' express from 1929, also changing to a Pullman service. Photograph by F.R. Hebron from Rail Archive Stephenson courtesy Rail-Online.

SOUTHERN
772

Above URIE N15 CLASS 4-6-0 – NO. 777
No. 777 *Sir Lamiel* is turned by manpower on an unidentified turntable in the early 1930s. The decade would see the increased use of vacuum motors to turn the locomotive utilising the vacuum connection at the front end. Also prominent is the 'E' prefix on the buffer beam, whereas 'No.' would have been more common. Photograph by C.R. Gordon Stuart from Rail Archive Stephenson courtesy Rail-Online.

Opposite URIE N15 CLASS 4-6-0 – NO. 772
Another view of no. 772 *Sir Percivale* when fitted with the large style smoke deflectors. The locomotive was erected by the NBLC in June 1925 and originally had a 5,000-gallon, eight-wheel tender. With the introduction of the 'Lord Nelson' Class 4-6-0s, there was an intention to have half of the ten ordered to be paired with 4,000-gallon, six-wheel tenders to work certain sections of the system. This was changed but the order remained the same and following construction the tenders were redistributed. Those built with the 'Lord Nelsons' went to N15 Class locomotives in an exchange, including no. 772 which has the tender here, in contrast to the previous image where the engine is running with one of the eight-wheel variety. Photograph courtesy Rail Photoprints.

URIE N15 CLASS 4-6-0 – NO. 766

No. 766 *Sir Geraint* passes Herne Hill with a southbound express in the 1930s. Photograph by B. Whicher from Rail Archive Stephenson courtesy Rail-Online.

Above URIE N15 CLASS 4-6-0 – NO. 763
Running through Bromley South during the 1930s is no. 763 *Sir Bors de Ganis*. The locomotive was another involved in tender exchanges and is seen here with a 4,000-gallon, six-wheel tender. Photograph by R.S. Clark from Rail Archive Stephenson courtesy Rail-Online.

Below URIE N15 CLASS 4-6-0 – NO. 795
New from Eastleigh Works in April 1926, no. 795 *Sir Dinadan* likely has been pictured around that date.

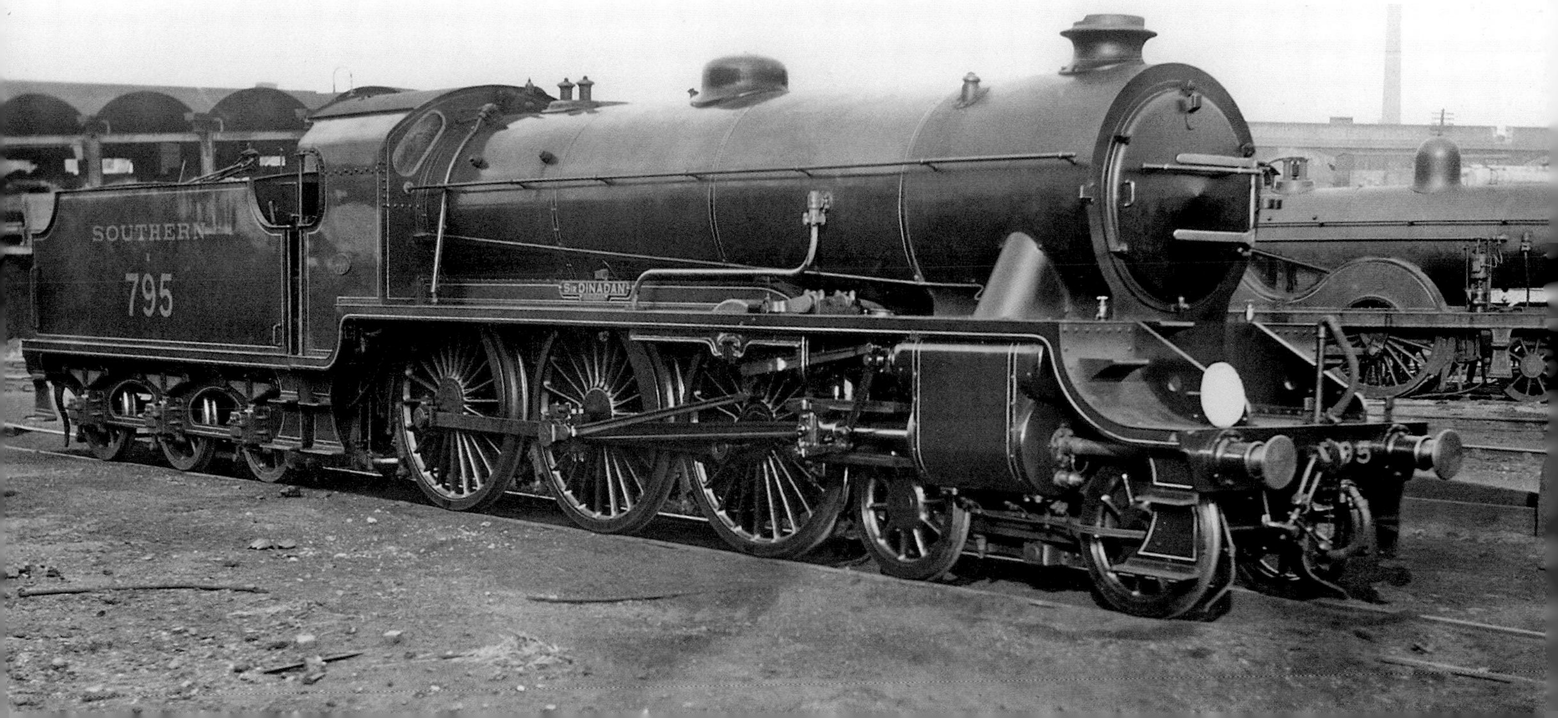

SPL
21
G
1
SOUTHERN

ROOMS
CELLARS
DEPOSITOR
SOUT
SIR ECTOR DE MARIS
SOUTHERN
794

Above MAUNSELL 'LORD NELSON' CLASS 4-6-0 – NO. 860

Following the successful trial of the first four-cylinder 4-6-0 – no. 850 *Lord Nelson* – in late 1926 and early 1927, an order for ten new locomotives was placed at Eastleigh Works. The original intention was to equip these with six-wheel, 4,000-gallon tenders, yet there was a change of plan and half received eight-wheel, 5,000-gallon tenders to increase their range. No. 860 *Lord Hawke* was the last of the first order built in April 1929. The locomotive is at what looks to be Nine Elms shed c. 1930. Photograph courtesy Rail-Online.

Opposite above URIE N15 CLASS 4-6-0 – NO. 769

In the late 1920s, no. 769 *Sir Balan* leaves Dover with a London-bound service. The engine has the standard smoke deflectors and retains the original 5,000-gallon tender with stepped-out sides. The latter was removed in December 1929 and switched with a straight-sided 5,000-gallon tender. Photograph courtesy Rail Photoprints.

Opposite below URIE N15 CLASS 4-6-0 – NO. 794

During May 1925, the SR ordered another 25 N15 Class 4-6-0s, though the number was later restricted to 14. These were built at Eastleigh Works and no. 794 *Sir Ector de Maris* was the second of the batch completed in March 1926. The locomotive appears to be in almost-new condition at Stewarts Lane shed in this image. The 14 engines were destined for ex-SE&CR lines and had six-wheel tenders from the start of service. There were also slight detail changes, including reduced firebox grate and higher heating surface in the boiler.

90

Above MAUNSELL 'LORD NELSON' CLASS 4-6-0 – NO. 857

Maunsell was constrained in producing more 'Lord Nelson' Class locomotives by the financial crisis of the late 1920s and early 1930s. This also affected planning for future designs and proposed classes remained on the drawing board. Yet, he was able to test certain features on a small scale and in mid-1936 an experimental boiler was ordered from Eastleigh Works. This had a round-top firebox which featured a combustion chamber and the barrel was constructed from nickel steel. During January 1937, no. 857 *Lord Howe* was fitted with the boiler and evaluated over the following years. Originally at Battersea shed, no. 857 moved to Nine Elms subsequently, but in November 1937 returned to Battersea to be tested on the Continental boat trains. The boiler was found to have poor circulation, resulting in steaming problems. With the installation of multiple blastpipes alongside other class members in 1938, the troubles improved slightly but the boiler was removed in 1941. Maunsell's successor, O.V.S. Bulleid used the boiler for testing thermic syphons in the firebox, which was a feature of his Pacifics, and this occurred from 1943 to 1945. No. 857 then returned to a standard boiler. The engine is pictured with a boat train at Chelsfield station during 1934. Photograph by H. Gordon Tidey from Rail Archive Stephenson courtesy Rail-Online.

Opposite MAUNSELL 'LORD NELSON' CLASS 4-6-0 – NO. 859

In service, the performance of the 'Lord Nelson' Class was found to be variable. Maunsell attempted to locate the problem and first tried to use smaller diameter driving wheels. No. 859 *Lord Hood* had a set fitted which had a diameter of 6 ft 3 in., reduced from the original 6 ft 7 in. No improvement was achieved and further investigations were necessary. No. 859 has a Victoria to Ramsgate train at Herne Hill station during the mid-1930s. Photograph by S.A.W. Harvey from Rail Archive Stephenson courtesy Rail-Online.

Nº 85

Above **MAUNSELL 'LORD NELSON' CLASS 4-6-0 – NO. 850**
When producing the design for the 'Lord Nelson' Class, Maunsell was restricted by the Civil Engineer into keeping the axle loads in certain limits to ensure the permanent way was safe. When the leading axle load breached this, Maunsell had to save as much weight as possible, leading to a drawn-out construction period. No. 850 *Lord Nelson* was ordered in June 1925 and did not appear until mid-August 1926. All expendable weight was removed during this period, resulting in heavily machined forged and cast components, slightly thinner frames, high-tensile steel motion components and lighter balance weights on the wheels. No. 850 ran around 10,000 miles under test, allowing the rest of the class to be completed. In 1938, the locomotive is pictured making a stop at Birchington on Sea station whilst at the head of a Victoria to Ramsgate service. Photograph by H. Gordon Tidey from Rail Archive Stephenson courtesy Rail-Online.

Opposite **MAUNSELL 'LORD NELSON' CLASS 4-6-0 – NO. 852**
Many of the 'Lord Nelson' Class locomotives were run-in when new from Eastleigh Works on secondary passenger trains to Bournemouth, then being dispatched to their London sheds. No. 852 *Sir Walter Raleigh* was noted as performing this task following completion in July 1928. The locomotive was first allocated to Nine Elms before moving over to Stewarts Lane where a partnership was formed with no. 853 *Sir Richard Grenville* on the depot's main duties. By the mid-1930s, no. 852 had returned to Nine Elms but was recorded as out of service for a time owing to changing traffic needs and several other class members were similarly affected. When in steam again, no. 852 was amongst a group working the Southampton and Bournemouth trains, including the 'Bournemouth Belle'. The locomotive has a train from London heading to the South Coast at Byfleet in 1938. Photograph by C.R.L. Coles from the Dave Cobbe Collection courtesy Rail Photoprints.

Below **MAUNSELL 'LORD NELSON' CLASS 4-6-0 – NO. 854**
Following Bulleid's arrival on the SR, a change was made to the livery of the express locomotives. The 'Lord Nelson' Class was repainted in malachite green with 'Southern' lettering on the tender in a new font and the locomotive number moved to the cab side. Whilst this was the standard, there existed some variations in lining colour and various parts that received either the livery or were painted black. No. 854 *Howard of Effingham* saw the first application in February 1939 when the malachite green was accentuated by black-and-white lining with the smoke deflectors black. From June 1939, the engine was one of a group running with black and yellow lining to the engine and smoke deflectors. Plain black with letters and numbers shaded green was the standard for the duration of the war and began in May 1942. No. 854 managed to retain the pre-war livery until March 1945, being the last repainted black. Green livery returned to the locomotive in June 1949 and no. 854 was the sole 'Lord Nelson' to use British Railways' prefix, being no. S854 from March 1948 to June 1949. The locomotive is at Stewarts Lane shed in March 1939. Photograph by C.R.L. Coles from the Dave Cobbe Collection courtesy Rail Photoprints.

Above MAUNSELL 'LORD NELSON' CLASS 4-6-0 – NO. 853

No. 853 *Sir Richard Grenville* takes the through road at Tonbridge whilst at the head of the 'Golden Arrow' express on 27th May 1939. The SE&CR traditionally ran an 11.00 express from Victoria station to Dover for a boat connection to the continent. The 1920s was the age of publicity and at the end of the decade the SR chose to name the service the 'Golden Arrow'. Originally, this was meant to be an exclusive service, being all Pullman carriages for first-class passengers. With the 1930s came the Depression and growing air travel, leading to the fall in passengers using the train. By 1931, a second class was in use, then the formation changed to just four Pullman coaches, six corridor vehicles and a pair of brake vans. Photograph by George C. Lander courtesy Rail Photoprints.

863
SOUTHERN

Opposite and above MAUNSELL 'LORD NELSON' CLASS 4-6-0 – NO. 863
Two images of no. 863 *Lord Rodney* under the attentions of a cleaning gang at Stewarts Lane shed during 1939. Around six months earlier, in mid-1938, no. 863 became the first 'Lord Nelson' Class member to be fitted with a Lemaître exhaust system. This followed an earlier attempt to improve the steaming of the class by fitting a Kylchap double blastpipe and chimney in August 1934. Even though crews and observers noted an improvement in performance by no. 862 *Lord Collingwood*, which was equipped, trials conducted measuring the fuel consumption recorded an increase, even though the two standard engines competing offered a discrepancy of 4 lb of coal burned per mile. Bulleid returned to the Kylchap arrangement in 1938 and introduced the Lemaître exhaust for comparison purposes. Over a number of tests, the latter was found most suitable, also being cheaper than the rival design. After tuning the arrangement, the Lemaître blastpipe had five nozzles which were 2⅝ in. diameter and the chimney was 2 ft 1 in. diameter. This was nearly three times larger than the original Maunsell design, significantly reducing back pressure in the cylinders and improving the draught through the firebox and boiler. The remainder of the class were dealt with in late 1938 and 1939. No. 863's chimney rim was initially quite plain, though this evolved as others were fitted and eventually the lip was substantial. Both photographs by C.R.L. Coles from Rail Archive Stephenson courtesy Rail-Online.

Above MAUNSELL 'LORD NELSON' CLASS 4-6-0 – NO. 856
Taking water at Southampton Central station whilst working the 'Bournemouth Belle' is no. 856 *Lord St. Vincent*. Photograph courtesy Rail-Online.

Opposite above MAUNSELL 'LORD NELSON' CLASS 4-6-0 – NO. 855
No. 855 *Robert Blake* is at New Malden station with a service bound for Bournemouth in 1946. Photograph by C.R.L. Coles from the Dave Cobbe Collection courtesy Rail Photoprints.

Opposite below MAUNSELL 'LORD NELSON' CLASS 4-6-0 – NO. 865
After the war, malachite green returned to the 'Lord Nelson' Class in April 1946. No. 865 *Sir John Hawkins* was the third repainted during June and is pictured in 1947 still looking presentable, with the smoke deflectors also having the livery. Photograph courtesy Rail Photoprints.

85
855
SOUTHERN

211
865
SOUTHERN
LOCO
31

MAUNSELL V 'SCHOOLS' CLASS
4-4-0 – NO. 914

No. 914 *Eastbourne* travels through Chelsfield station during the 1930s. Photograph by H. Gordon Tidey from Rail Archive Stephenson courtesy Rail-Online.

Above MAUNSELL V 'SCHOOLS' CLASS 4-4-0 – NO. 900

No. 900 *Eton* stands at Charing Cross station when new in 1930. The engine entered traffic from Eastleigh Works during March. Photograph by W.J. Reynolds from Rail Archive Stephenson courtesy Rail-Online.

Below MAUNSELL V 'SCHOOLS' CLASS 4-4-0 – NO. 904

No. 904 *Lancing* is at New Cross Gate shed in the early 1930s.

Opposite above MAUNSELL V 'SCHOOLS' CLASS 4-4-0 – NO. 905

Approaching Tonbridge with a service from London Bridge is no. 905 *Tonbridge*. Seen on 27th May 1939, the engine was nearly ten years old and had entered service without smoke deflectors. This was the case for the first order and subsequent 'Schools' had them fitted from new. Photograph by George C. Lander courtesy Rail Photoprints.

Opposite below MAUNSELL V 'SCHOOLS' CLASS 4-4-0 – NO. 935

Bulleid's first foray into the application of streamlining concerned 'Schools' Class no. 935 *Sevenoaks*. In February 1938, the locomotive had plywood panels fixed to the exterior to create a possible publicity opportunity for the 'Bournemouth Limited'. Renumbered 999, the streamlining lasted only a short time and was removed following a solitary main line test from Eastleigh to Micheldever. No. 935 returned to service in late March 1938.

Below MAUNSELL V 'SCHOOLS' CLASS 4-4-0 – NO. 934

Three orders for Maunsell's V Class 4-4-0, commonly referred to as the 'Schools', were placed in the late 1920s and early 1930s. The final one, E496, was placed in March 1932 and consisted of 20 locomotives, yet this was subsequently curtailed to just ten. No. 934 *St. Lawrence* was delivered from Eastleigh Works in March 1935. The locomotive has posed for a portrait around that time.

33
SOUTHERN
905
№ 905

SOUTHERN
SOUTHERN
999

381
927
SOUTHERN
232
8 7
92

Above MAUNSELL V 'SCHOOLS' CLASS 4-4-0 – NO. 918

Following his success improving the steaming of the 'Lord Nelson' Class, Bulleid turned to the 'Schools' Class even though the performance of the locomotives was quite satisfactory. In February 1939, no. 914 *Eastbourne* was fitted with a Lemaître blastpipe and stovepipe chimney. Despite trials indicating no particular advantage, authorisation was given for another 19 class members to be altered. No. 918 *Hurstpierpoint* was one of four to be altered during June 1940. By 1941, the expense of the alterations was deemed unnecessary owing to the war and further conversions ceased. No. 918 has reached Tonbridge with a London Bridge to Hastings express on 27th May 1939. Photograph by George C. Lander courtesy Rail Photoprints.

Opposite MAUNSELL V CLASS 'SCHOOLS' 4-4-0 – NO. 927

As Bulleid was finalising his new passenger livery, four 'Schools' Class locomotives were at Eastleigh Works and returned to traffic repainted in malachite green with black-and-white lining on the boiler, cylinders and tender. The smoke deflectors were black in this instance, though later in 1939 class members appeared with them coloured malachite green. No. 927 *Clifton* was part of both groups, entering traffic from repair in early July 1938, then having the deflectors decorated in the first half of 1940. In the latter instance the lining applied was black and yellow, with unlined cylinders. No. 927 is at Waterloo station with an express to Bournemouth around July/August 1938 in the first version of Bulleid's livery. Photograph by O.J. Morris from Rail Archive Stephenson courtesy Rail-Online.

S R
SOUTHERN
915
No 91
396
© John P. Wilson/
Rail Archive Stephenson

Above MAUNSELL V 'SCHOOLS' CLASS 4-4-0 – NO. 911

Approaching Tonbridge with a London Bridge to Hastings train on 27th May 1939 is no. 911 *Dover*. Still in Maunsell livery, the locomotive had around a year left before Bulleid's malachite green with black and yellow lining was applied, including to the smoke deflectors. Bulleid was said to have disliked Maunsell's green as being too dull, but apart from improving the appearance, the malachite shade was also cheaper by around £6. No. 911 was amongst the engines fitted with a Lemaître exhaust which occurred during October 1940. Photograph by George C. Lander courtesy Rail Photoprints.

Opposite MAUNSELL V 'SCHOOLS' CLASS 4-4-0 – NO. 915

When sent into traffic during March 1933, no. 915 *Brighton* became one of a quartet of 'Schools' Class at Eastbourne shed. From there, the engines were used on services to London Bridge and Victoria stations. When this route was electrified, the group transferred to Bricklayers Arms shed, London, finding use on ex-SE&CR lines. Later in the 1930s, 12 were at St Leonards, 12 Ramsgate, 10 Fratton and the remainder worked from Bricklayers Arms. No. 915 is with 11.15 express from Charing Cross to Dover and Deal on 14th July 1939. Photograph by John P. Wilson from Rail Archive Stephenson courtesy Rail-Online.

MAUNSELL V 'SCHOOLS' CLASS 4-4-0 – NO. 902

In July 1946, no. 902 *Wellington* is at Tonbridge with an express. Photograph from the David P. Williams Archive.

Above MAUNSELL V 'SCHOOLS' CLASS 4-4-0 – NO. 904
New in May 1930, no. 904 *Lancing* has a train at Clapham Junction station around a year later. A truck behind the engine is carrying a horse-drawn removal van.

Below MAUNSELL V 'SCHOOLS' CLASS 4-4-0 – NO. 924
At an unidentified shed for servicing is no. 924 *Haileybury*. The locomotive was paired with a 4,000-gallon tender when new and this was capable of carrying 5 tons of coal.

SOUTHERN
21C1
CHANNEL PACKET
MERCHANT NAVY CLASS
SOUTHERN
21C1

SOUTHERN
21C3
ROYAL MAIL
MERCHANT NAVY CLASS
21C3
SOUTHERN

SOUTHERN
21C11
21C 11

Above BULLEID 'MERCHANT NAVY' CLASS 4-6-2 – NO. 21C9
No. 21C9 *Shaw Savill* is on the through line at Berrylands station with a West England express in 1942/1943. The Lemaître exhaust is discharging plenty of smoke and the blastpipe was similar to that fitted to the 'Lord Nelson' Class. The original front end design is present, though this would later change. Photograph courtesy Rail-Online.

Opposite above BULLEID 'MERCHANT NAVY' CLASS 4-6-2 – NO. 21C1
The SR went against the other 'Big Four' companies by putting their faith in electrification and during the inter-war years, this was a successful move as the rise of the commuter began. Yet, when the Second World War loomed, the SR had to adapt and introduce a new steam class which would ultimately facilitate a successful transition to a fully electric system. Bulleid received authorisation for the new class in March 1938 and initially there were to be 20, but this increased to 30. Ambitiously, Bulleid wanted to construct a 4-8-2, though the design was rejected as too heavy and rigid. He then turned to the 4-6-2 or Pacific wheel arrangement and incorporated as many unusual features as possible. By this time, the war was underway and the first 'Merchant Navy' Class Pacific was delayed until mid-February 1941. The locomotive, no. 21C1 *Channel Packet,* is pictured when returned to malachite green livery after the war.

Opposite middle BULLEID 'MERCHANT NAVY' CLASS 4-6-2 – NO. 21C3
The first 'Merchant Navy' Class Pacific was in service for around three months before joined by no. 21C2 *Union Castle*, then another three before no. 21C3 *Royal Mail* was ready during September 1941. The engine is in works grey livery for this photograph taken at the time.

Opposite below BULLEID 'MERCHANT NAVY' CLASS 4-6-2 – NO. 21C11
The initial five 'Merchant Navy' Class Pacifics were completed in malachite green livery with yellow bands, though the finish was matt rather than gloss. This soon weathered and helped show imperfections in the casing sheets, leading to black being standard for new engines. No. 21C11 *General Steam Navigation* was completed on 31st December 1944 as the first locomotive of the second batch which incorporated detail differences from the initial run.

SOUTHERN

21C105

Above BULLEID 'MERCHANT NAVY' CLASS 4-6-2
On the SR, both Maunsell and Bulleid consulted with footplate crews to ascertain the optimum layout in the cab. The 'Merchant Navy' Class had several labour-saving features, though some did not last the lifespan of the locomotives. A steam generator provided electric lighting for gauges, reverser, cut-off indicator and injectors. The casing around the motion and oiling points was also lit to improve servicing. A small steam cylinder opened the firebox door by means of a pedal on the floor. Small holes were drilled in the door which allowed the door to be closed during intense periods of activity. Both injectors were on the fireman's side, whereas traditionally one would have been at the driver's side. The cab was also quite enclosed as the tender front was built up to the cab roof height giving maximum protection from the elements. This did provide a problem during warmer spells as the cab could become sweltering.

Opposite above BULLEID 'MERCHANT NAVY' CLASS 4-6-2 – NO. 21C5
With the problems arising from the matt paint, no. 21C5 *Canadian Pacific* entered service in malachite green livery but was returned to Eastleigh and repainted black before the official naming ceremony took place in March 1942. As the war drew to a conclusion, the SR was keen to reintroduce the standard passenger livery. With the second group of ten 'Merchant Navy' Class under construction, no. 21C12 *United States Lines* brought the return of malachite green and the first batch were dealt with between December 1945 and August 1947. No. 21C5 was repainted in January 1946 and the livery is distinct in this image from around that time as the engine reaches Salisbury. Photograph courtesy Rail-Online.

Opposite below BULLEID 'WEST COUNTRY' CLASS 4-6-2 – NO. 21C105
A dedicated express locomotive for West England services was necessary as the war started, with T9 4-4-0s and N Class 2-6-0s the principal motive power. An order for 20 had been placed at Brighton in April 1941, yet no design was prepared and the first provisional one did not appear until December 1942. Bulleid originally envisaged a 2-6-0, then 2-6-2 and finally a 4-6-2 Pacific to meet an expanded role for an express engine where electrification was postponed. This design had to be lighter than the 'Merchant Navy' Class and changes included shorter length (including tender), fabricated components and smaller boiler. The construction number rose from 20 to 30 and these were delivered between May 1945 and May 1946. An early locomotive from the batch, no. 21C105, later named *Barnstaple*, is in the Erecting Shop at Brighton Works on 12th July 1945, with another class member in front awaiting a boiler. No. 21C105 was in traffic by the end of the month. Photograph by Wilfred Beckerlegge from Rail Archive Stephenson courtesy Rail-Online.

© C.R.L. Coles/
Rail Archive Stephenson

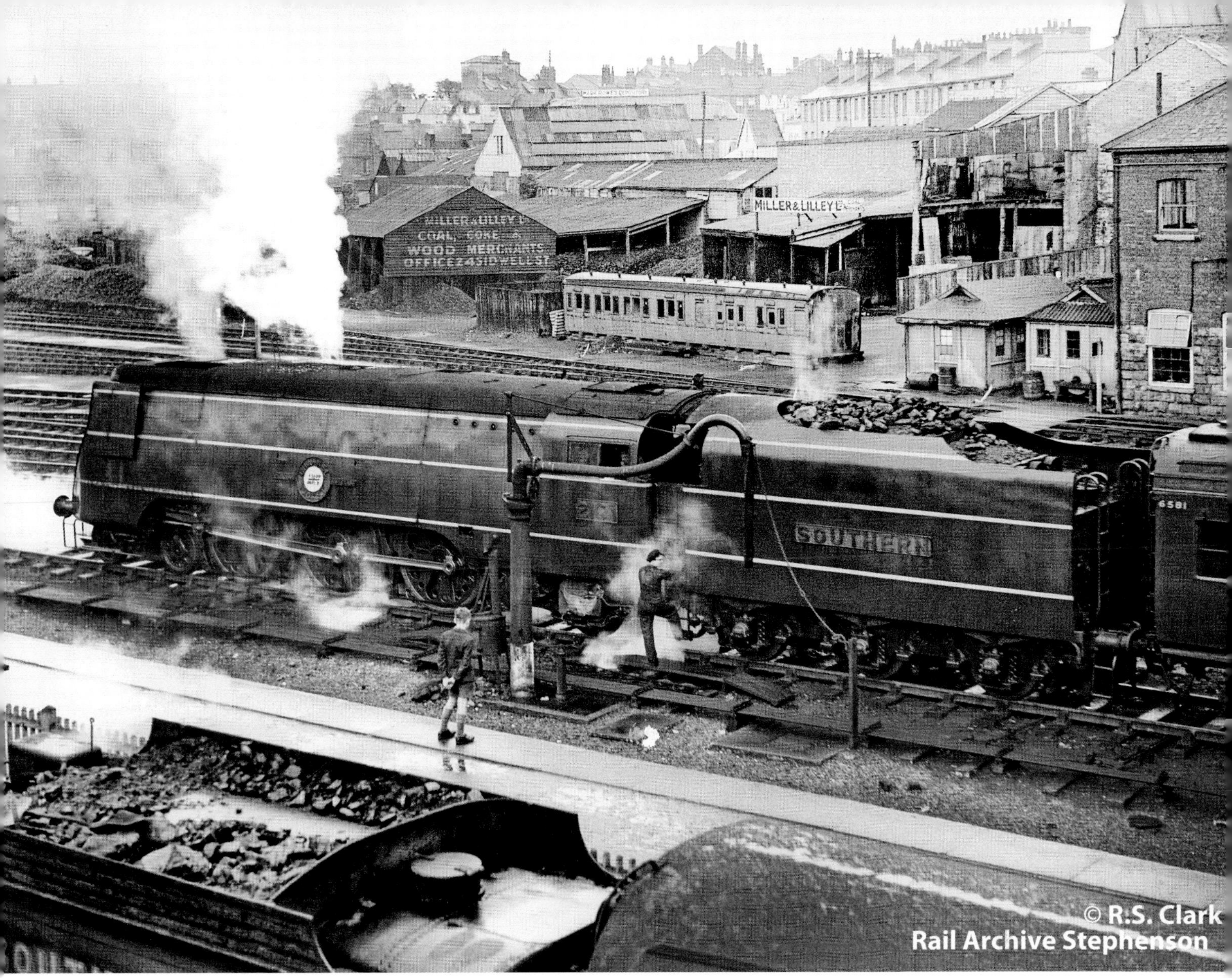

Above BULLEID 'MERCHANT NAVY' CLASS 4-6-2 – NO. 21C1

The 'Merchant Navy' Class locomotives were paired with a 5,000-gallon tender capable of carrying 5 tons of coal. These were built at Ashford Works as the shops had welding equipment which was employed in the construction process. The six wheels were the Bulleid Firth Brown-type in line with the other wheelsets. These disc wheels were developed to reduce hammer blow, fit the tyre more efficiently and distribute weight evenly. Just visible in this image of no. 21C1 *Channel Packet*, the cab side sheets are of the original design ending just past the window. After complaints of draughts, the sheets extended much further into the cab to give better protection. No. 21C1 is at Exeter Central station uncoupling carriages on the middle road during 1946. Photograph by R.S. Clark from Rail Archive Stephenson courtesy Rail-Online.

Opposite BULLEID 'WEST COUNTRY' CLASS 4-6-2 – NO. 21C119

On 15th April 1946, the 'Golden Arrow' service was reinstated, dispensing with 'Lord Nelson' Class 4-6-0s and began using the Bulleid Pacifics. In the summer of that year, no. 21C119 – named *Bideford* in August – has drawn the attention of several travellers at Victoria station. The departure time was 10.00 and an allowance of one hour forty minutes was given to reach Dover Marine. Photograph by C.R.L. Coles from Rail Archive Stephenson courtesy Rail-Online.

21C124
SOUTHERN
5
© Rail Archive Stephenson

Above BULLEID 'WEST COUNTRY' CLASS 4-6-2 – NO. 21C103

The 'Merchant Navy' Class suffered problems with exhaust drifting towards the cab and this was partially addressed with the hood in front of the chimney. With the introduction of the 'West Country' Pacifics, continued incidents resulted in extra plates being fitted to the smokebox side sheets. The arrangement was standard from February 1947 and no. 21C103 *Plymouth* shows this following modification.

Opposite BULLEID 'WEST COUNTRY' CLASS 4-6-2 – NO. 21C124

Unnamed 'West Country' Pacific no. 21C124 leaves Victoria station with an express for Ramsgate via Chatham on 18th April 1946. The locomotive was subsequently named *Tamar Valley*. Photograph from Rail Archive Stephenson courtesy Rail Online.

BULLEID 'WEST COUNTRY' CLASS 4-6-2 – NO. 21C124

Still to be named 'West Country' no. 21C124 has a Charing Cross to Ashford train at Sevenoaks station in 1946. Photograph by A.W. Croughton from Rail Archive Stephenson courtesy Rail-Online.

Above BULLEID 'BATTLE OF BRITAIN' CLASS 4-6-2 – NO. 21C164

The vast majority of the Bulleid 'West Country' and 'Battle of Britain' Pacifics were constructed at Brighton. No. 21C164 is outside the shops during July 1947 and has works grey livery. The locomotive was named *Fighter Command* subsequently. Photograph by Wilfred Beckerlegge from Rail Archive Stephenson courtesy Rail-Online.

Below BULLEID 'MERCHANT NAVY' CLASS 4-6-2 – NO. 21C14

In the yard at Eastleigh shed during the mid-1940s is 'Merchant Navy' Class no. 21C14 *Nederland Line*. The locomotive is fitted with the short smoke deflectors and a longer version later became standard.

SOUTHERN
35
THE
BOURNEMOUTH
BELLE
21C159
SOUTHERN
PULLMAN

Left BULLEID 'MERCHANT NAVY' CLASS 4-6-2 – NO. 21C19

As built, the first two 'Merchant Navy' Class engines had the 'Southern' plates on the smokebox door cast in a horse shoe shape. After some objections this changed to a circular plate which usefully incorporated the construction information. They also had metal numberplates whereas later class members did not receive them. The second batch of ten engines were built with short smoke deflector plates, as well as the hood in front of the chimney. No. 21C19, later *French Line CGT*, has been pictured around May 1945.

Opposite page BULLEID 'BATTLE OF BRITAIN' CLASS 4-6-2 – NO. 21C159

On 16th July 1947 no. 21C159 is prepared to leave with the 'Bournemouth Belle' service. The engine had been in traffic since March and was later named *Sir Archibald Sinclair*. Photograph by J.P. Wilson from Rail Archive Stephenson courtesy Rail-Online.

Below BULLEID 'MERCHANT NAVY' CLASS 4-6-2 – NO. 21C2

No. 21C2 *Union Castle* is at Semley station with a West England express in the mid-1940s. The engine's metal number plates, as well as 'Southern' on the tender, are still in use, though the smokebox plate is the second version and the additional smoke deflectors are present. Photograph courtesy Rail Photoprints.

THE
BOURNEMOUTH
BELLE
35
21C13
SOUTHERN

Above **BULLEID 'MERCHANT NAVY' CLASS 4-6-2 – NO. 21C12**

No. 21C12 *United States Lines* was the first engine of the second batch to receive malachite green livery when painted in April 1945 for an official naming ceremony. The locomotive had been in service since January and was new to Nine Elms shed. The 'Merchant Navy' Class members there were mainly used on the Bournemouth expresses and no. 21C12 has reached Bournemouth Central station with a service in the mid-1940s. Photograph courtesy Rail-Online.

Opposite **BULLEID 'MERCHANT NAVY' CLASS 4-6-2 – NO. 21C13**

The LSWR introduced Pullman carriages on the Bournemouth route, adding a Drawing Room Car to four afternoon trains in each direction. These later fell out of use and Pullman services did not return to Bournemouth expresses until 1931. This was named the 'Bournemouth Belle' and was initially Sunday-only, though at the start of 1936 became daily and ran non-stop for a time before calling at Southampton. In the mid-1940s, 'Merchant Navy' Class no. 21C13 *Blue Funnel* passes Clapham Junction with the southbound 'Bournemouth Belle'. Photograph courtesy Rail Photoprints.

442
SOUTHERN
21 C 10
VIROL
HAMPTONS
PALL MALL LONDON S.W.1
FURNITURE CARPETS
ALL GOODS CARRIAGE PAID

Above BULLEID 'MERCHANT NAVY' CLASS 4-6-2 – NO. 21C19

Withdrawn when the Second World War started, the 'Bournemouth Belle' returned on 7th October 1946. There were ten Pullman carriages (three first class, seven thirds, seating 66 and 236 respectively) in the train which had a two-hour schedule between Waterloo and Bournemouth, with a stop at Southampton included. The train left the capital at 12.30 with a scheduled arrival at Bournemouth West at 14.46, whilst the reverse departed at 19.15 for entry to Waterloo around 21.25. From 1947, the timetable changed and the train from Bournemouth left at 18.45. No. 21C19 *French Line CGT* is at Vauxhall with the 'Bournemouth Belle' during the mid-1940s. Photograph courtesy Rail-Online.

Opposite BULLEID 'MERCHANT NAVY' CLASS 4-6-2 – NO. 21C10

Approaching the SR station at Basingstoke is no. 21C10 *Blue Star* which has an express from Waterloo heading westward. To the extreme left, the GWR's line to Reading and signal box can be seen. No. 21C10 was rebuilt in January 1957 and was in traffic for a further nine years before withdrawn. Photograph from the David P. Williams Archive.

OTHER SR LOCOMOTIVE CLASSES

Above MAUNSELL U1 CLASS 2-6-0 – NO. 1907
Taking the through line at Tonbridge on 27th May 1939 is Maunsell U1 Class no. 1907. The locomotive was one of 21 three-cylinder 2-6-0s built for passenger services from 1928 to 1931. Photograph by George C. Lander courtesy Rail Photoprints.

Opposite above MAUNSELL N CLASS 2-6-0 – NO. 1406
On shed at Exmouth Junction in September 1933 is Maunsell N Class no. 1406. The locomotive was just eight months old at this time and went on to be in traffic for over 30 years. Photograph courtesy Colour-Rail.

Opposite below DRUMMOND K10 CLASS 4-4-0 – NO. 388
Outside the depot at Feltham during August 1929 is Drummond K10 Class 4-4-0 no. 388. The locomotive was amongst a group of five built for the LSWR in 1902. A total of 40 entered service for the company in the early 20th century and the engines were used on mixed duties. Photograph courtesy Colour-Rail.

SOUTHERN
1406

822

SOUTHERN
863

Above MAUNSELL N CLASS 2-6-0 – NO. 819

The efficiency of the steam locomotive was a constant concern of railway engineers. Energy expended in creating steam and still present in the exhaust was wasteful. Attempts were made to recycle this by using the steam to preheat the feedwater before entering the boiler. Several devices were developed in the early 20th century, including the Worthington feedwater heater which mixed exhaust steam from the cylinders and the heater pump to raise the temperature of the water before returned into the boiler. The apparatus was installed on Maunsell N Class no. 819 in December 1924 and ran with the locomotive to April 1927 when removed. In that period, no. 819 has been caught at an unidentified location.

Opposite above MAUNSELL N1 CLASS 2-6-0 – NO. 822

In 1914, Maunsell began planning for the N Class 2-6-0 in order to eliminate some of the older classes working on the SE&CR system. Because of the war, the prototype did not appear until 1917 and a production batch was not completed until 1920. In the meantime, Maunsell became interested in a three-cylinder locomotive to improve the power available for traffic requirements. With the SE&CR having line restrictions, the use of three cylinders presented design challenges and these were met by Harold Holcroft who devised a method of working the inside cylinder valves using the outside set. The first N1 Class locomotive, no. 822, was completed after Grouping in 1923 and then tested against representatives of constituents' classes. Following mixed results, no further examples were ordered until the late 1920s when another five appeared from Ashford Works during 1930. These had boiler modifications and the valve gear altered so a separate set of Walschaerts motion operated the centre cylinder. No. 822 is pictured in works grey livery after construction in 1923.

Opposite below MAUNSELL N CLASS 2-6-0 – NO. 863

After extensive trials with the first N Class 2-6-0, the SE&CR ordered another 15 locomotives in 1919. The Ministry of Supply manufactured 100 kits of components for the design following the First World War and these were later made available for purchase. The SR obtained 50 of these, whilst the Metropolitan Railway bought some others, as did the Midland Great Western Railway of Ireland. The 50 SR locomotives, except the boilers, were initially fabricated by the Royal Arsenal, Woolwich, then assembled at Ashford Works. No. 863 was amongst the group and entered traffic during May 1925.

Rail Archive Stephenson

Above **BILLINTON K CLASS 2-6-0 – NO. 2346**
Just before the First World War, the LB&SCR needed a versatile locomotive that could be used on freight traffic, then called upon for passenger services when necessary. Billinton devised the K Class 2-6-0 which featured a Belpaire firebox, Weir feedwater heater, Robinson superheater and Stephenson motion. Two were ordered initially in 1913 and proved successful. Further examples followed and up to Grouping 17 locomotives were erected. No. 2346 was amongst a batch completed during the First World War. The engine is at Havant in December 1938. Photograph by C.R.L. Coles from the Dave Cobbe Collection courtesy Rail Photoprints.

Opposite above **URIE H15 CLASS 4-6-0 – NO. 475**
A Salisbury to Waterloo train has been caught near Pirbright in the mid-1940s with Urie H15 Class no. 475 at the head. The H15s survived Nationalisation and the first class member was withdrawn in 1955. Lasting over several years, the process ended in 1961 and no. 475 was amongst the nine left that were sent to the scrapyard. Photograph from Rail Archive Stephenson courtesy Rail-Online.

Opposite below **URIE H15 CLASS 4-6-0 – NO. 476**
Urie took over from Drummond on the LSWR in the early 1910s and found the stock in need of modernisation. His first design was the H15 Class 4-6-0 which was robust and simple. Urie also conducted trials with superheating for the first batch, built in 1914, but found these did not meet his requirements and introduced the Eastleigh superheater as a result. After Grouping, Maunsell ordered another 15 to meet immediate traffic needs and no. 476 was amongst this group when completed during 1924. The engine has a London-bound milk train at Raynes Park on 10th September 1926. Photograph by F.R. Hebron from Rail Archive Stephenson courtesy Rail-Online.

SOUTHERN
847

Above URIE S15 CLASS 4-6-0 – NO. 497
Urie developed his H15 Class 4-6-0 to cover LSWR freight duties. In 1920 and 1921, four orders of five locomotives were placed at Eastleigh Works. After Grouping, several improvements were made to the design under Maunsell and 15 new S15s were built. Before his retirement, the last batch of ten entered service with further detail differences. No. 497 was the first class member built in March 1920. The locomotive is in the yard at Feltham shed during September 1928. Photograph by W. Boyden courtesy Colour-Rail.

Opposite above MAUNSELL N CLASS 2-6-0 – NO. 847
To increase line capacity, the SE&CR saw a need to operate longer freight trains. With this added weight, a suitable locomotive was necessary. Maunsell produced the N Class 2-6-0 which could handle the traffic. Between 1917 and 1934, 80 locomotives were produced and spread across the system. No. 847 was assembled at Ashford Works in February 1925.

Opposite below BILLINTON C2 CLASS 0-6-0 – NO. 436
In the early 1890s, Billinton produced an improved 0-6-0 for LB&SCR freight traffic. The first ten were ordered from Vulcan Foundry and appeared in 1893. The manufacturer was subsequently tasked with providing a further 45 C2 class members and these were delivered up to 1902. D.E. Marsh introduced his own 0-6-0 with larger boiler – C3 – during 1906 and he later fitted this to C2 Class locomotives. A total of 29 engines were altered, becoming C2X, before the programme was discontinued. No. 436 remained to C2 specifications throughout 57 years in service. The engine is at Newhaven in September 1930. Photograph courtesy Colour-Rail.

Above MARSH C3 CLASS 0-6-0 – NO. 2304
On shed at Norwood Junction in April 1936 is Marsh C3 no. 2304. The locomotive's career of 30 years was to end in July. Photograph by W. Boyden courtesy Colour-Rail.

Below STIRLING O1 CLASS 0-6-0 – NO. 1066
O1 Class no. 1066 is in store at New Cross Gate shed. Originally part of the O Class, a new boiler fitted in May 1916 took the engine into the O1 Class. The locomotive later resumed service and was condemned during 1951.

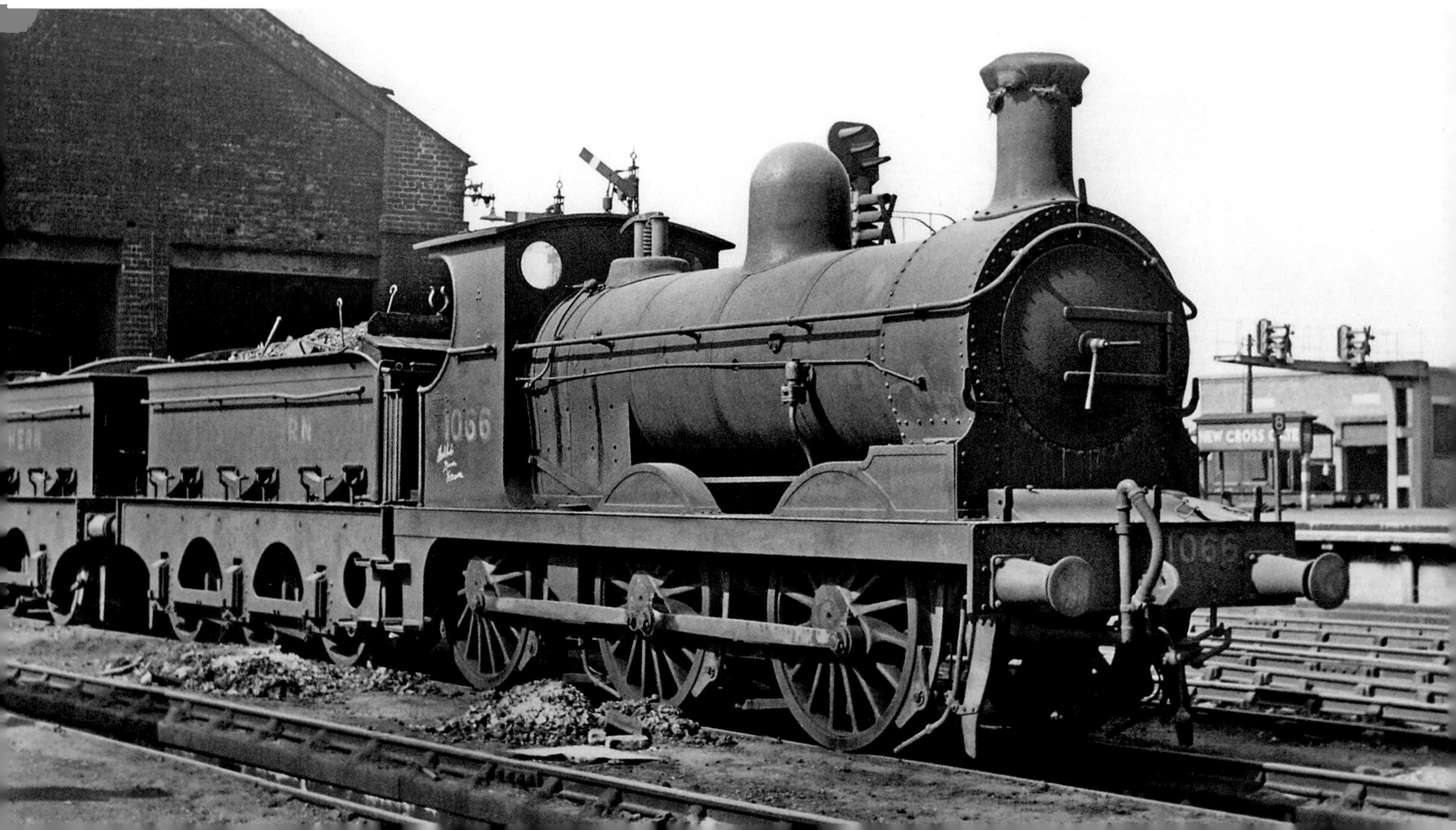

Above ADAMS A12 CLASS 0-4-2 – NO. 643
In September 1933, Adams A12 Class no. 643 is seen at Exmouth Junction shed. Built by Neilson & Co., the engine was in service from March 1893 to July 1947. Photograph by W. Boyden courtesy Colour-Rail.

Below WAINWRIGHT C CLASS 0-6-0 – NO. 1593
A short mixed freight takes a platform line through Tonbridge station on 27th May 1939. The locomotive is Wainwright C Class no. 1593. Photograph by George C. Lander courtesy Rail Photoprints.

Above MAUNSELL Q CLASS 0-6-0 – NO. 530

Shortly before he left office, Maunsell addressed a need for a freight locomotive with the Q Class. Twenty were ordered when Bulleid took over and he allowed them to be completed, though later fitted Lemaître exhaust systems to the class. No. 530 was the first to be built in January 1938.

Below MAUNSELL Z CLASS 0-8-0T – NO. 951

For shunting duties in the SR's important marshalling yards, Maunsell designed the Z Class 0-8-0T in the late 1920s. Eight engines were produced, including no. 951 which is at Hither Green during the 1930s. Photograph from the David P. Williams Archive.

Above BILLINTON C2X CLASS 0-6-0 – NO. 547

In 1908, D.E. Marsh fitted a C3 boiler to a Billinton C2 Class locomotive and found improved performance. Of the 55 C2s, 45 became C2X engines up to the Second World War. No. 547 was modified early in 1908. The locomotive is pictured at Bognor during June 1933. Photograph by W. Boyden courtesy Colour-Rail.

Below MAUNSELL Q CLASS 0-6-0 – NO. 545

Maunsell Q Class no. 545 entered service in June 1939 and was new to Nine Elms shed. The engine was later loaned, amongst others, to Southampton for special services. Later in the war, no. 545 was noted at Guildford.

C 15
C 15

Above BULLEID Q1 CLASS 0-6-0 – NO. C1

Bulleid foresaw the need for a simple, reliable and robust freight locomotive soon after the start of World War Two. Initially favouring a 2-6-0, he changed to an 0-6-0 that was devoid of unnecessary features to improve maintenance and reduce materials consumed. Forty Q1 Class engines were built at Brighton and Ashford Works in 1942. The unconventional appearance was the result of using Idaglass, a fibreglass insulating material that could not tolerate any weight stresses. No. C1 was new in March 1942 and tested from Brighton to Three Bridges or Worthing, then dispatched to Guildford shed. The locomotive is seen when new at Brighton.

Opposite BULLEID Q1 CLASS 0-6-0 – NO. C15

View towards the goods yard at Chichester during 1947. Q1 Class no. C15 is with a mixed freight train. When new, the engine was one of ten Q1s allocated to Eastleigh shed, displacing a similar number of Maunsell Q Class 0-6-0s. At Nationalisation, no. C15 was again noted as working from Eastleigh. The locomotive was in service to November 1964. Photograph by C.R.L. Coles from the Dave Cobbe Collection courtesy Rail Photoprints.

Reginald S. Clark/Rail Archive Stephenson

Above DRUMMOND M7 CLASS 0-4-4T – NO. 322

For suburban services around London, several railway companies favoured the 0-4-4T wheel arrangement in the late 19th century. On the LSWR, William Adams introduced the T1 Class in 1888 and over several years 50 of the design were built. At the turn of the century, suburban London was developing and increased demand for services meant a new locomotive was necessary. Drummond, who took over in 1895, stuck to the 0-4-4T type but increased the boiler pressure and changed firebox arrangements. Twenty-five M7 Class engines from Nine Elms Works appeared in 1897 and a steady stream of orders followed to 1911 when 105 had been completed. No. 322 was the first of five from Nine Elms during 1900. In the mid-1920s, the locomotive is at Barnstaple Junction.

Opposite LYNTON & BARNSTAPLE RAILWAY 2-6-2T – NO. 188

Though four narrow gauge locomotives were at work on the Lynton & Barnstaple Railway, the SR thought another was necessary following Grouping. Manning Wardle, which supplied three of the original quartet in the late 1890s, was approached for a locomotive of a similar design to the earlier group, though with some modifications. No. 188 *Lew* was delivered in 1925 and worked to the end of the line in 1936. Being newer than the other engines, no. 188 was saved from being scrapped and in the sale of equipment and stock from the L&BR was purchased by a plantation in Brazil. The locomotive is seen with a crew at Barnstaple shed during the late 1920s. Photograph by Reginald S. Clark from Rail Archive Stephenson courtesy Rail-Online.

SOUTHERN
2326
737

SOUTHERN
791
RIVER ADUR

Above MARSH I1X CLASS 4-4-2T – NO. 596
Twenty I1 Class 4-4-2Ts were built at Brighton Works in 1906 and 1907 for local services. These locomotives developed a reputation for poor performances and Maunsell reacted by fitting a boiler used by B4 4-4-0s and I3 4-4-2Ts. This was successful and the whole class was dealt with from 1925 to 1932, being reclassified I1X. No. 596 was erected in November 1906, then rebuilt during July 1925. The locomotive is seen at an unidentified location during the late 1920s. Photograph courtesy Rail Photoprints.

Opposite above MARSH J2 CLASS 4-6-2T – NO. 2326
Shortly before his retirement for ill health, D.E. Marsh designed a 4-6-2T locomotive to work the most important expresses between London and Brighton. J1 Class no. 325 was built in late 1910 and following six months of trials, a second engine, no. 326, was ordered during May 1911. Just two months later Marsh resigned and Billinton modified the J1 being built to use Walschaerts valve gear in place of the Stephenson motion employed by no. 325. The change reclassified no. 326 as a J2. Both locomotives worked their intended role to the mid-1920s when replaced by new classes. Remaining on the Brighton line to 1935, the pair was used elsewhere on the SR network to the early 1950s when condemned for scrap. No. 2326 has been caught at an unidentified location during the 1930s. Photograph courtesy Rail Photoprints.

Opposite below MAUNSELL K CLASS 2-6-4T – NO. 791
The permanent way of both the LC&DR and SER was of particularly poor character and greatly restricted axle loads permissible on those lines. Following Maunsell's appointment, he needed to address express passenger matters, as loads were increasing and double heading was often necessary. Initially proposing a new 4-4-0, Maunsell had to change to a 2-6-4T which would suit all requirements. In January 1915 an order for six K Class locomotives was placed at Ashford Works, though their erection became delayed due to the war. In the event, only one engine from the order, no. 790, appeared and the remainder cancelled. A new order for ten was placed in 1920 and components began to be assembled but no complete locomotive was ready before Grouping. Maunsell affirmed the order in 1925 and the first, no. 791 *River Adur*, was delivered from Armstrong Whitworth & Co. in May. On 24th August 1927, K Class no. 800 *River Cray* derailed, resulting in the deaths of 13 and many injuries. The design of the locomotive was given as a cause of the accident due to several factors. In response, the SR rebuilt all K Class 2-6-4Ts as U Class 2-6-0s. No. 791 was converted at Eastleigh Works during July 1928.

SOUTHERN
B
596
10

65
SOUTHERN
249

Above MARSH I1X CLASS 4-4-2T – NO. 600
No. 600 is on shed at Brighton during the mid- to late 1920s. The locomotive was erected at the nearby works in March 1907. Rebuilding to I1X Class specifications took place 20 years later. No. 600 went on to be the first class member withdrawn during October 1944. The remaining I1X engines mostly left service in 1948 and 1951.

Opposite above MARSH I1X CLASS 4-4-2T – NO. 596
The LB&SCR opened the first locomotive shed at Horsham in February 1848. South of North Street, then named Crawley Road, the straight shed had three tracks that led to a turntable. By the turn of the century, this was inadequate and moved to land north of Crawley Road. The building was a roundhouse and a coal stage and water tank were built as well. Under the LB&SCR, Horsham was the top depot in the district but declined in importance to Nationalisation. Marsh I1X Class no. 596 is on the depot's turntable in July 1927. During the year, the turntable was upgraded from 46 ft diameter to 55 ft diameter as the apparatus from Orpington was relocated. Photograph by W. Boyden courtesy Colour-Rail.

Opposite below DRUMMOND M7 CLASS 0-4-4T – NO. 249
No. 249 was amongst the first 25 members of the Drummond M7 Class. These had the frames projecting just a short distance in front of the leading wheels, whereas those built from 1900 had the frame length increased. Originally, the front sandboxes were part of the splashers, but these also moved from this year to several places before returning to the initial position. No. 249 has stopped at Addison Road station, Kensington, with a passenger train. The locomotive was amongst 20 M7s withdrawn in 1963 which left 13 in service and all were condemned during the following year.

MARSH I1X CLASS 4-4-2T – NO. 2602

Around 1930, I1X Class no. 2602 stands outside Littlehampton shed. The engine had been rebuilt during December 1926.

Above STROUDLEY D1 CLASS 0-4-2T – NO. 2260
Brookwood station had a bay platform for travellers to the nearby Brookwood Cemetery. Stroudley D1 Class no. 2260 is in the bay during the 1930s. Traffic to the cemetery ceased in April 1941.

Below BILLINTON E4 CLASS 0-6-2T – NO. 2508
Travelling along the Brighton to Southampton line near Ford, is E4 Class 0-6-2T no. 2508. The locomotive was erected in 1900 and had a career lasting 60 years. Photograph from the David P. Williams Archive.

SOUTHERN
2595
705

Above MARSH J2 CLASS 4-6-2T – NO. 2326

Receiving attention at Eastleigh Works during the early 1930s is Marsh J2 Class no. 2326. Around 1924, the locomotive's name was removed and from that time used just the number, no. 326. Originally, instead of *Bessborough*, the engine was to carry the name 'Grosvenor'. Renumbered under BR to 32326 in May 1948, another three years passed before withdrawal.

Opposite above MARSH I1X CLASS 4-4-2T – NO. 2595

There were some slight variations over the 18-month construction period of Marsh's I1 Class. No. 595 was the first built in September 1906 and had external copper piping. The locomotive, and the following two, also had a lower water capacity at 1,839 gallons, whilst later ones saw this raised to 1,924 gallons. The last ten had wheelsets and motion fitted that were recycled from withdrawn classes which caused a reduction in wheelbase. No. 595, renumbered 2595 in the early 1930s, was rebuilt to I1X specifications during January 1927. The engine has a passenger train at London Bridge.

Opposite below STROUDLEY A1X CLASS 0-6-0T – NO. 647

For traffic into the outlying areas of London, Stroudley introduced the A1 Class 0-6-0T in 1872. Following the initial order for six, another 44 engines were built to 1880. Amongst these was no. 647, which appeared from Brighton Works in December 1876 as no. 47 *Cheapside*. The locomotive ran to the early 20th century before renumbered 647 and the name was removed as the LB&SCR wanted new designs to have lower numbers. Like many other older classes, the A1s were rebuilt with new boilers. D.E. Marsh started the process in 1911 and 16 became A1X Class members to Grouping. No. 647 was dealt with during January 1912. Under the SR, a small number of A1Xs survived working on local lines and branches. No. 647 managed to see Nationalisation but a broken axle saw the engine scrapped in October 1951. The locomotive and crew pose at Brighton during September 1930. Photograph by W. Boyden courtesy Colour-Rail.

ADAMS 415 CLASS 4-4-2T – NO. 3125

Built by Robert Stephenson & Co. in 1885, Adams 415 Class no. 3125 was originally condemned in 1929. Employed on the Axminster to Lyme Regis branch at the time, replacement engines failed and no. 3125 returned to service, managing another 30 years. The locomotive is at the branch bay platform during the mid-1930s. Photograph by Reginald S. Clark from Rail Archive Stephenson courtesy Rail-Online.

Above BEATTIE 0298 CLASS 2-4-0WT – NO. 3314
Between duties at Wadebridge, c. 1935, is Beattie 0298 Class no. 3314. Photograph courtesy Rail Photoprints.

Below STROUDLEY D1 CLASS 0-4-2T – NO. 2252
D1 Class no. 2252 entered service as no. 252 *Buckhurst* in 1882. The locomotive went on to be one of the last class members in service when condemned during 1950. No. 2252 is seen at an unidentified location before Nationalisation. Photograph from the David P. Williams Archive.

SOUTHERN
232
No 232

SOUTHERN
94
SOUTHERN
100

Above USA CLASS 0-6-0T – NO. 63

The United States Army Transportation Corps built a large number of shunting locomotives, Class S100, for use in the European and North African theatres during 1942. Spreading out on to various systems as the Allies advanced, many were later bought after the conflict ended. On the SR, the B4 Class was becoming life expired by the 1940s and Bulleid looked to the S100s now surplus in storage. One was taken on trial and found acceptable, leading to a total of 15 being bought in 1946-1947. Amongst this number was no. 63 which was erected at Vulcan Iron Works, Wilkes-Barre, Pennsylvania, in 1942. The engine is in Eastleigh Works during October 1947 being refurbished before entering service. Photograph from Rail Archive Stephenson courtesy Rail-Online.

Opposite above STROUDLEY D1 CLASS 0-4-2T – NO. 232

Appearing after the A1 Class, Stroudley's D1 Class 0-4-2T locomotive was produced for services heavier than the aforementioned could handle. As a result, the boiler pressure was higher at 150 lb per sq. in., compared with 140 lb per sq. in. of the A1s, and the driving wheel diameter was 5 ft 6 in. From 1873 to 1887, 125 engines were erected by Brighton Works (90) and Neilson & Co. (35). No. 232 was a product of Brighton Works in July 1884, being named *Lewes* at the time, though this was later removed. Around 1930, no. 232 has been pictured at Bere Alston station. The locomotive later became no. 2232 and was withdrawn during June 1944.

Opposite below ADAMS B4 CLASS 0-4-0T – NO. 94

For LSWR dock shunting operations, Adams designed the B4 Class 0-4-0T in 1891. The coal bunkers were located within the cabs, whilst the cylinders were outside the frames and the motion was placed inside. Ten were completed initially at Nine Elms Work, including no. 90 shown here. Two years later, a second batch appeared and no. 100, which is behind no. 90, was amongst this number. Under Drummond, the last group of five B4s were built. No. 90 and no. 100 are in Plymouth Friary shed on 8th May 1937. The two were withdrawn in 1948 and 1949 respectively. Photograph courtesy Colour-Rail.

Above **BILLINTON E5 CLASS 0-6-2T – NO. 2592**

R.J. Billinton used the 0-6-2T wheel arrangement to meet traffic requirements in several areas. Developing Stroudley's F Class design, his first engines of the type belonged to the E3 Class which was used on freight and shunting duties. As these were capable, Billinton increased the wheel diameter and boiler pressure to create a mixed traffic 0-6-2T. Classified E4, 75 appeared between 1897 and 1903. The final version of the type was the E5 and still larger wheels were fitted, along with a boiler from the C2 Class. The first was built in 1902 and another 29 followed before construction halted during 1904. No. 2592 was new from Brighton Works during April 1904 as no. 592 *Eastergate*. In 1947, no. 2592 is running through Chichester with a local freight. The engine was employed for another six years before condemned. Photograph by C.R.L. Coles from the Dave Cobbe Collection courtesy Rail Photoprints.

Opposite above **MARSH I3 CLASS 4-4-2T – NO. 2082**

D.E. Marsh's 4-4-2T designs from the early 20th century suffered from a flaw in the firebox design. The I1, I2 and I4 Classes struggled on assigned duties as a result. When finally enlarging the firebox for the I3 Class of 1907, the steaming was much improved and further orders were placed. Initially, two had been built, one being standard and the other fitted with a Schmidt superheater. Though no clear advantage was displayed at the time, of the next ten engines ordered, four had superheaters. These did show an economy and the final 15 I3s constructed were fitted with superheaters from new. No. 2082 was one of these when built at Brighton during August 1914. The locomotive is departing from Havant with a Portsmouth to Brighton train in 1938. Photograph by C.R.L. Coles from the Dave Cobbe Collection courtesy Rail Photoprints.

Opposite below **STIRLING R1 CLASS 0-6-0T – NOS 1337 AND 1340**

The line to Folkestone Harbour fell at a 1 in 30 gradient and the heavy boat trains required assistance to depart. Three locomotives are at work here in 1946, with the two leading engines identifiable as Stirling R1 Class 0-6-0Ts nos 1337 and 1340. Photograph courtesy Rail Photoprints.

SOUTHERN
2082
722

E 22
£1000

ELECTRIC

Above 'BRIGHTON BELLE' PULLMAN 5-BEL EMU – NO. 3051
For the start of electric services on the mainline between Victoria and Brighton, the SR offered a Pullman service. Three sets of five carriages were built by Metropolitan Cammell Carriage & Wagon Co. during 1932 and began operating in 1933 as the 'Southern Belle' service until mid-1934 when the title changed to the 'Brighton Belle'. The sets were initially numbered 2051-2053 but from January 1937 the running numbers became 3051-3053. No. 3051 is pictured after this date, running through Merstham, north of Redhill. Photograph by O.J. Morris from Rail Archive Stephenson courtesy Rail-Online.

Opposite LONDON & SOUTH WESTERN RAILWAY ELECTRIC – NO. E22
The railways dominated the Victorian era, yet as this came to an end, so did the monopoly on public transport. Around London, tramways, initially horse-drawn, adopted electric power in the early 1900s and became immediately popular, being cheap to use and relatively fast. As the 1910s began, action was necessary on the LSWR and the new General Manager, Herbert Ashcombe Walker, sought to improve services whilst making economies in operation and maintenance of the suburban trains. Whereas the Midland Railway and LB&SCR had tested overhead electric systems, the LSWR investigated the use of a third rail and found this both cheap and reliable. In 1913, the company began a scheme to electrify the lines from Waterloo to Hounslow, Waterloo to Kingston upon Thames, the main line to Hampton Court Junction and two branches from there to Hampton Court and Claygate. Amounting to 50 route miles, the estimate cost was over £1 million. The first section to Wimbledon via East Putney was ready in late 1915, followed by the Kingston line in early 1916, Hounslow during March and to Hampton Court by the end of the year. This scene was captured at Hounslow station, c. 1920, with a three-carriage Electric Multiple Unit, no. E22, stopped for passengers whilst on a Waterloo to Hounslow and Richmond service. By 1920, passenger numbers on the electrified lines were said to have increased by 25 million. Photograph by F.H. Stingemore from Rail Archive Stephenson courtesy Rail-Online.

Above 6-PUL EMU – NO. 2001

With the Brighton electrification scheme progressing, the SR planned new stock for express services. Two power cars were ordered from contractors – Birmingham Railway Carriage & Wagon Co. and Metropolitan Cammell Carriage & Wagon Co. – whilst three trailers were repurposed from obsolete stock. Set no. 2001 was formed and tested in the early 1930s. A driver is at the controls of the power car here.

Above **5-BEL EMU – NO. 2053**

In July 1934, 5-BEL set no. 2053 is at Patcham. The formation was Driving motor brake third parlour, two Trailer parlour first with kitchen, Trailer parlour third, Driving motor brake third parlour. Photograph by O.J. Morris from Rail Archive Stephenson courtesy Rail-Online.

Below **3-SUB EMU – NO. 1677**

Stood at St Mary Cray station in the 1930s is 3-SUB no. 1677. The set was three vehicles formed from redundant LSWR stock in 1927/1928. Photograph by A.W. Croughton from Rail Archive Stephenson courtesy Rail-Online.

Above **4-BUF EMU BUFFET CAR**

In July 1938, the electrification of the line from Three Bridges to Portsmouth was completed. New sets were provided for Victoria to Portsmouth services, numbering 13 and featuring buffet cars. The interior of one is seen here.

Above EMU FIRST-CLASS COMPARTMENT

Dating from 1935, this image shows the interior of a first-class compartment from a contemporary EMU. This is possibly the 6-PAN set built during the year for express services on newly electrified lines, of which several were dealt with at the time. The formation consisted of a Driving motor third brake open, Trailer corridor third, Trailer corridor first, Trailer corridor first and pantry, Trailer corridor third and Driving motor third brake open. These sets were often paired with a 6-PUL to increase capacity.

Above left FIRST-CLASS COMPARTMENT 2-HAL EMU – NO. 12814

The last electrification schemes completed before the war were from Gravesend to Strood and Maidstone West, Swanley to Gillingham and Otford Junction to Maidstone East. For these routes, a large number of two-car units were assembled at Eastleigh Works. These 2-HAL pairs consisted of Driving trailer composite and Motor brake third. The interior of DTC no. 12814 is above left and there were four first-class compartments, 7 ft 2 in. wide, whilst there were also four third-class compartments, 6 ft 3 in. wide. Seating was for a total of 24 firsts and 32 thirds. No. 12814 was paired with MBT no. 10778 and together formed set no. 2660 which entered service in May 1939 and lasted to May 1971.

Above right FIRST-CLASS COMPARTMENT 2-BIL EMU – NO. 12073

Following on from the success of the first ten 2-BIL units, further examples appeared for new schemes. When the one from Portsmouth to Bognor Regis reached completion, 68 sets were assembled, consisting of Driving motor brake third with lavatory and Driving trailer composite with lavatory. Carriage no. 12073, with first-class compartment illustrated, belonged to the latter classification and the Driving motor brake third paired was no. 10616. Both were connected as set no. 2050 and were in service to January 1971.

Opposite THIRD-CLASS SALOON 6-PAN EMU

The Driving motor brake third open carriages were built by the Birmingham Railway Carriage & Wagon Co. and Metropolitan Cammell Carriage & Wagon Co. in equal numbers. Made from metal sheets and box girder underframes, the vehicles were 66 ft 2¾ in. long, weighed 59 tons and had seating for 52 third-class passengers, with a small smoking section provided. The saloon is shown opposite.

Above 4-COR EMU – NO. 3149

Two 4-COR sets have been paired together for this Victoria to Portsmouth service which is passing Mickleham, near Dorking, during 1939. No. 3149 is the leading unit and was new in March 1938. The set was originally made up of a Driving motor brake open third (no. 11215), Trailer corridor third (no. 10103), Trailer corridor composite (no. 11839), Driving motor brake open third (no. 11216). Early in the war, the last two coaches were damaged in an air raid and were replaced. Photograph by O.J. Morris from Rail Archive Stephenson courtesy Rail-Online.

Opposite above FIRST-CLASS COMPARTMENT 2-HAL EMU – NO. 12809

2-HAL EMU Driving trailer composite no. 12809 was built in May 1939 and coupled to Driving motor brake third no. 10773, forming set no. 2655. The interior of a first-class compartment is shown opposite.

Opposite below 4-BUF EMU BUFFET CAR

Thirteen buffet car sets were built in mid-1938. The buffet carriage itself had 26 seats, ten of which were in front of a bar and the remainder in a saloon around stylised tables. Pullman Car Co. personnel worked the buffet until 1942 when refreshment facilities were withdrawn from services. The 4-BUF sets then operated as three units until January 1946. A saloon is illustrated here.

12809 C

SOUTHERN

THIRD

ISLE OF WIGHT

Above ISLE OF WIGHT CENTRAL RAILWAY 2-4-0T – NO. W5
The Isle of Wight Central Railway was formed in 1886 as three of the island's companies grouped together. One of these was the Ryde & Newport Railway, which opened during 1875 and amongst the locomotives acquired around this time was no. W5. Built by Beyer, Peacock & Co. in May 1876, the 2-4-0T was new to the line as no. 6, though was renumbered no. 5 by the IWCR and named *Osbourne*. The locomotive is at Newport station after Grouping and before April 1926 when withdrawn. Photograph by R.S. Clark from Rail Archive Stephenson courtesy Rail-Online.

Opposite above BULLEID/RAWORTH CO-CO ELECTRIC – CC1
With an extensive network of electric lines, the SR turned to plans for electric locomotives. Bulleid and the Chief Electrical Engineer Alfred Raworth worked together on a bogie electric locomotive with third-rail pick-up apparatus. Two prototypes were built during the war and numbered CC1 and CC2, whilst a third, CC3, with detail differences appeared after Nationalisation. The locomotives had six traction motors generating nearly 1,500 horsepower and were capable of hauling both passenger and freight trains weighing nearly 1,000 tons. Though mainly operating from the third-rail, a pantograph was provided for when the locomotives were in marshalling yards. The presence of a live rail in these areas was obviously too dangerous for employees.

Opposite below ELECTRIFICATION AT LITTLEHAMPTON
Distinguished gentlemen pose for the camera as they celebrate the opening of the electric line to Littlehampton on 30th June 1938. The electrification of the Brighton to Portsmouth line followed on from the main line scheme to Portsmouth which had cost £3 million. The first mentioned was completed in stages as the first section operated from Brighton to West Worthing in 1933, then in 1938 to Havant, including the branches to Littlehampton and Bognor. The official opening was the date above, yet the public did not have access until 2nd July. Littlehampton station was to be rebuilt but the war delayed this and a new facility was not constructed until 1987.

VENTNOR

Above ISLE OF WIGHT RAILWAY 2-4-0T – *BONCHURCH*
The final locomotive taken into Isle of Wight Railway stock was Beyer, Peacock & Co. 2-4-0T *Bonchurch*. Built in April 1883, the engine was absorbed by the SR and became W18 until condemned during May 1928. This event was four years away when the locomotive was pictured arriving at Ventnor station with a train from Ryde Pier Head. Photograph by F.R. Hebron from Rail Archive Stephenson courtesy Rail-Online.

Opposite above ISLE OF WIGHT RAILWAY 2-4-0T – *VENTNOR*
Though proposed in the mid-1840s, the Isle of Wight Railway did not receive an Act of Parliament until 1860. The company opened the first section of line from Ryde to Sandown in 1864 and two years later had an extension to Ventnor completed. A branch from Brading to Bembridge was built independently but operated by the IWR later in the 19th century. The company initially used three 2-4-0T locomotives and gradually increased the stock. *Ventnor* was added to the group in October 1868 when purchased from Beyer, Peacock & Co. After Grouping, the engine was numbered W15 but this only lasted to September 1925 when withdrawn. *Ventnor* is at Ventnor with a crew c. 1920. Photograph by H. Gordon Tidey from Rail Archive Stephenson courtesy Rail-Online.

Opposite below ISLE OF WIGHT CENTRAL RAILWAY 0-6-0T – NO. 10
LB&SCR A1 Class 0-6-0T no. 69 *Peckham* was amongst a number of class members withdrawn in the early 20th century but sold on to other railways or private concerns. In April 1900, the locomotive was taken on a hire purchase agreement with the Isle of Wight Central Railway, becoming no. 10 in their stock list. The engine survived to Grouping and has been pictured during August 1923 near Smallbrook Junction with a Medina Wharf to Ryde train. No. 10 became W10 *Cowes* and was also rebuilt to A1X specifications in 1930. The locomotive was withdrawn in May 1936. Photograph by B. Whicher from Rail Archive Stephenson courtesy Rail-Online.

Above ISLE OF WIGHT RAILWAY 2-4-0T – W13 *RYDE*

Bembridge was virtually cut off from the mainland of the Isle of Wight by Brading Marshes. Many schemes had been formulated to drain and reclaim the land but the first successful one did not arrive until the late 19th century. Started in 1864, over the next 14 years some 800 acres were reclaimed at a cost of over £400,000. The authorisation of the work also gave provision for the construction of a harbour with pier at Bembridge. As the project progressed, thoughts turned to connecting with the Isle of Wight Railway at Brading and in 1874 an Act was given for a 2½-mile branch to Bembridge. Built independently, the route was worked by the IWR which later purchased the operation before the end of the 19th century. Bembridge station opened during May 1882 and had one platform, a single running line and two siding lines for goods and coal trains. The crew of this local train to Brading has stopped for the camera, c. 1930. The locomotive is 2-4-0T no. W13 *Ryde* which left traffic in 1932. Photograph by R.S. Clark from Rail Archive Stephenson courtesy Rail-Online.

Below ISLE OF WIGHT RAILWAY 2-4-0T – NO. W8
The Cowes & Newport Railway reached Newport in June 1862, whilst the Ryde & Newport Railway was not completed until 1875. At this time, the latter company established an engine shed at Newport, north of the station, with two roads and a water tank. Later, a coal stage was added and the facilities were used to the late 1950s. During 1927, 2-4-0T no. W8 is on site. The locomotive was built by Beyer, Peacock & Co. in May 1898 and ran nameless throughout the 30 years spent in traffic. No. W8 was sent for scrap during November 1929. Photograph by O.J. Morris from Rail Archive Stephenson courtesy Rail-Online.

SOUTHERN
W
13
RYDE

SOUTHERN
2
YARMOUTH

Above **STROUDLEY A1X CLASS 0-6-0T – NO. W12**
Caught at Newport is Stroudley A1X Class no. W12. Built in September 1880 as the last class member, the locomotive was LB&SCR no. 84 *Crowborough*. Sold to the IWCR in 1903, the company had the engine, then no. 12, rebuilt to A1X during the First World War and service continued to May 1936.

Opposite above **ISLE OF WIGHT RAILWAY 2-4-0T – NO. W13 *RYDE***
The development of the railway system on the Isle of Wight was mainly concentrated in the north and east of the island. On the west side, a scheme was proposed in the late 1860s, yet failed to gain support. The Freshwater, Yarmouth & Newport Railway received authorisation in 1880, with backing from the LSWR which operated a ferry service to Yarmouth. The project progressed slowly, owing to lack of money and avoidance of difficult engineering works. Goods services began in 1888 and passenger trains during 1889. In the mid-1920s, no. W13 *Ryde* has one of the route's services here at Newport station. Originally worked by the Isle of Wight Central Railway, strained relations before the First World War led to the FY&NR to retake control and operate the trains. As a result, a new station opened at Newport and this lasted to Grouping when the SR unified the system. No. W13 was in service to July 1932.

Opposite below **STROUDLEY E1 CLASS 0-6-0T – NO. W2 *YARMOUTH***
As Stroudley's E1 Class became surplus to requirements on the mainland, a quartet was sent to the Isle of Wight. No. 152, originally named *Hungary*, relocated in the summer of 1932 and became no. W2 *Yarmouth*. The number had been vacated a short time earlier by Stroudley A1 Class 0-6-0T no. W2 *Freshwater* which was also rebuilt to A1X specifications. No. W2 *Yarmouth*, and the other E1s, were mainly to be used on freight services, but following some modifications to the wheel balance could be found hauling passenger trains. The locomotive, which is seen at Newport, was condemned in October 1956.

Above STROUDLEY A1X CLASS 0-6-0T – NO. W13 *CARISBROOKE*
No. W13 *Carisbrooke* stands at Ryde St Johns Road shed. The locomotive was originally no. W3, but became no. W13 during 1932. In April 1949, the locomotive left the island and was renumbered to no. 32677.

Below ADAMS O2 CLASS 0-4-4T – NO. W32 *BONCHURCH*
No. W32 *Bonchurch*, with Bulleid livery, is light engine at Ryde Pier Head station.

Above ISLE OF WIGHT RAILWAY 2-4-0T – NO. W16 *WROXALL*
No. W13 *Wroxall* is at Bembridge station during 1928. The locomotive was delivered to the IWR in April 1872 and remained active until June 1933.

Below ADAMS O2 CLASS 0-4-4T – NO. W30 *SHORWELL*
Built in September 1892, LSWR no. 219 arrived on the Isle of Wight during April 1926, becoming no. W30 *Shorwell*. The engine is between duties at Ryde St Johns Road shed. Withdrawal occurred during September 1965.

SOUTHAMPTON DOCKS

Above ADAMS B4 CLASS 0-4-0T – NO. 176
To serve Southampton Docks, a number of shunting locomotives were necessary. Adams B4 Class 0-4-0Ts worked there for many years and no. 176 *Guernsey* is seen around the time of Grouping. Photograph by Reginald S. Clark from Rail Archive Stephenson courtesy Rail-Online.

Opposite above DRUMMOND C14 CLASS 0-4-0T – NO. 0741
Drummond's C14 Class 2-2-0 was an attempt to offer greater flexibility to the railmotor concept popular in the early 20th century. Proving underpowered for this role, Urie started a programme to rebuild them as 0-4-0Ts. Interrupted by the war, many were disposed of to the Ministry of Munitions for employment shunting. Three of ten C14s remained at Grouping, with no. 0741 amongst the trio and the engine had been rebuilt in March 1922. Water is being taken by the locomotive at Southampton Docks, c. 1925. Photograph by W.V. Wiseman from Rail Archive Stephenson courtesy Rail-Online.

Opposite below DRUMMOND F9 CLASS 4-2-4T – NO. 58S
For travelling around the LSWR system, Drummond produced the F9 Class 4-2-4T, no. 733, in 1899. Falling into disuse after his death, the inspection saloon was reinstated as no. 58S in the early 1930s to conduct people around the works for the New Dock at Southampton. The saloon is there with an additional carriage during June 1932. Photograph by O.J. Morris from Rail Archive Stephenson courtesy Rail-Online.

V.V. Wiseman/
l Archive Stephenson

S R
58S

CLAUSENTUM
SOUTHERN
1618

69
SOUTHERN

Above 0458 CLASS 0-4-0ST – NO. 3458
One of two 0458 Class members was no. 3458 *Ironside* which is pictured c. 1940.

Opposite above 0458 CLASS 0-4-0ST – NO. 734
No. 734 *Clausentum* was built for the Southampton Dock Co. in 1890. The locomotive is seen c. 1930.

Opposite below USA CLASS 0-6-0T – NO. 69
Outside the small shed provided for dock locomotives at Southampton is USA Class no. 69.

Below ADAMS B4 CLASS 0-4-0T – NO. 90
In 1934, Adams B4 Class no. 90 *Caen* poses with enginemen and railway staff at Southampton. Photograph from the David P. Williams Archive.

CARRIAGES

7383
SOUTHERN
RAILWAY
7383
FIRST
FIRST

4171
SOUTHERN
RAILWAY
4171
SECOND
SECOND

Above COMPOSITE CARRIAGE – NO. 9600

For the Victoria to Orpington and Holborn to Shortlands electrification scheme of 1925, the SR had contractors build new motor and trailer sets. The latter group was sourced from the Birmingham Railway Carriage & Wagon Co. and were diagram 758 composite carriages for 20 third-class and 56 first-class passengers. Coach no. 9600 is pictured and was placed in set no. 1509, though owing to delays, the carriage originally ran in a four-car formation.

Opposite above and below 'CONTINENTAL' SET CARRIAGES – NO. 7383 AND NO. 4171

The SE&CR was ready to introduce new vehicles for continental traffic just before the First World War began. Maunsell took up the task after the conflict and was authorised to build a train of eight carriages catering for first-class and second-class passengers. The vehicles had generous proportions and were the largest built by the company at the time. Two more sets were ordered by the SE&CR before Grouping and these appeared in late 1923. Proving suitable for the travellers bound for the ports at Folkestone and Dover, more sets were desired immediately and these had to be ordered from the trade. Consisting of 41 carriages, the order was split between the Metropolitan Carriage & Wagon Co. and the Birmingham Railway Carriage & Wagon Co. This batch differed slightly from earlier examples by having increased dimensions and the formation consisted of a brake third, whereas the class had been omitted previously. Two of the coaches built by the BRC&WC are illustrated here. Opposite above is first-class carriage no. 7383 which was a diagram 496 vehicle with 6½ compartments. Opposite below is second-class coach no. 4171 and this was built to diagram 235, with 7½ compartments provided.

9600
SOUTHERN
RAILWAY
9600
3
3

5142
SOUTHERN
RAILWAY
5142
THIRD
THIRD
THIRD
FIRST
FIRST
FIRST
FIRST

SOUTHERN RAILWAY
DINING SALOON

Above **ROYAL SALOON**
In line with other railway companies, the SE&CR decided to assemble a new set for Royal train duties following the accession to the throne of King Edward VII and Queen Alexandra. Whilst some existing carriages were refurbished, the Royal Saloon was built specifically and ordered from the Lancaster Railway Carriage & Wagon Co., which soon after became part of the Metropolitan Amalgamated Railway Carriage & Wagon Co., and delivered during 1903. Initially numbered 1R, under the SR the number was 7930. The interior of the saloon is shown and the colour scheme was green with mahogany furniture and panelling. The set was used during the reign of Edward VII and George V, then falling out of use during the late 1930s. Other important dignitaries also utilised the formation. Interestingly, the Royal Saloon was later converted into a camping coach and was last used in Scotland before condemned during 1970.

Opposite top **COMPOSITE CARRIAGE – NO. 9600**
Another view of composite carriage no. 9600. There were nine compartments provided, with the third-class placed at either end. These were 5 ft 8 in. wide, whilst the first-class passengers had 7 ft 0¾ in. compartments. Four of the seven first-class compartments allowed smoking.

Opposite middle **COMPOSITE CARRIAGE – NO. 5142**
With constituent orders being built immediately after Grouping, a short period elapsed where the new SR carriage stock could be developed. Amongst the features made standard were the use of Buck-eye couplers and Pullman gangways, as well as underframe length of 57 ft 11 in., and body length 58 ft (from corner to corner). In 1925 new carriages were ordered for South Coast services and those to the West of England. Composite carriage no. 5142 was constructed at this time to diagram 2301 and was part of a set destined for use on the London to Plymouth route.

Opposite below **FIRST-CLASS DINING SALOON – NO. 7861**
A group of six first-class dining saloons with kitchens were built in 1927. These were intended to be used on services to Bournemouth and Portsmouth on the route from Waterloo. No. 7861 was one of the six and is seen when new. There were four groups of seats in the vehicle, a pantry and the kitchen.

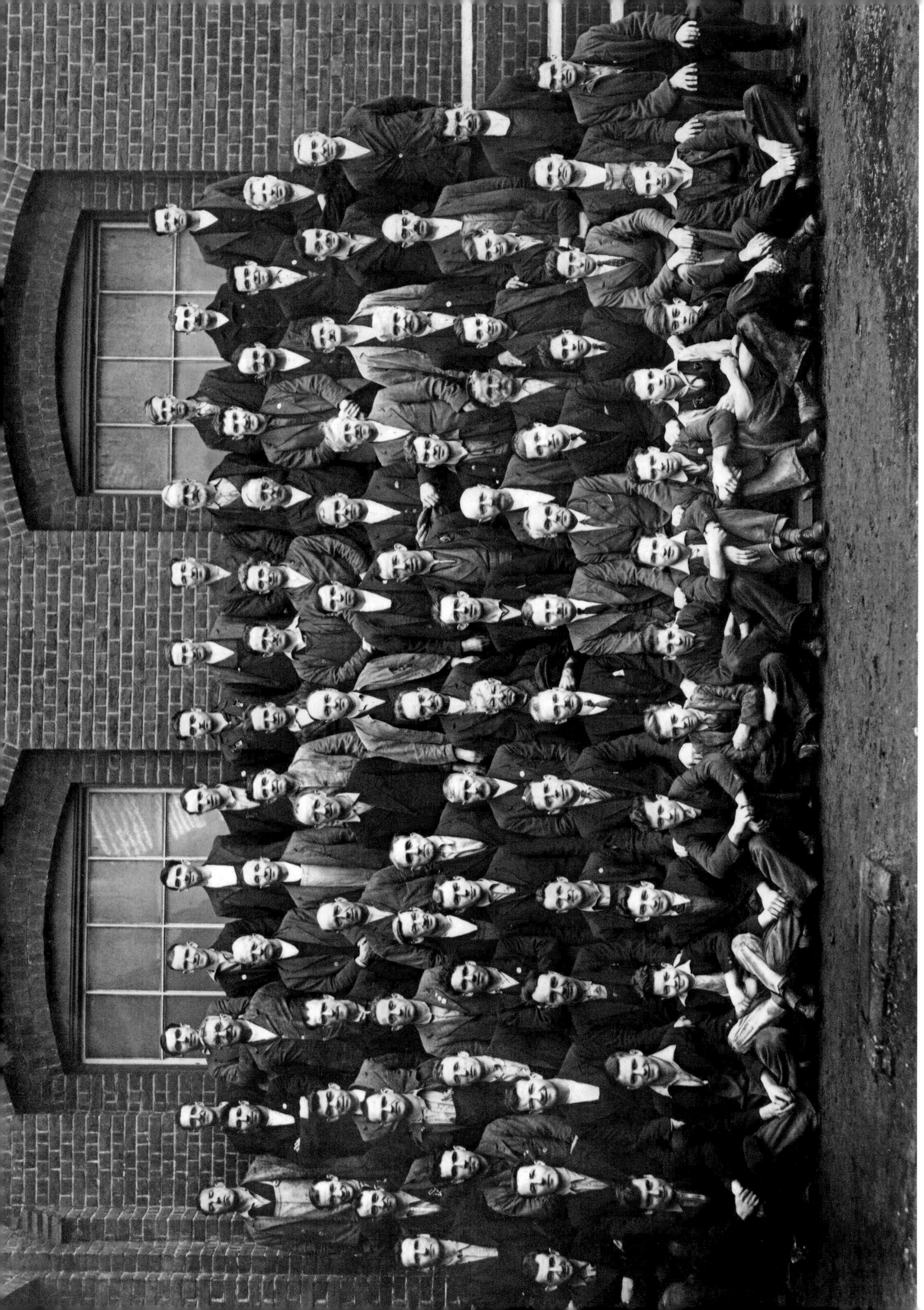

Above RESTAURANT CARRIAGE
Interior of an SR catering vehicle.

Opposite EASTLEIGH WORKS
Staff from the carriage and wagon department at Eastleigh Works sit for this photograph from November 1937.

Below GENERAL SALOON – NO. 4448
The continental boat train stock required flexibility in the formations and some carriages were unclassified. No. 4448 was built in the early 1930s and had seating for 36, with a brake compartment also present.

Above THIRD-CLASS OPEN SALOON

Forty-one diagram 2007 third-class open saloons were built in 1936. Just two years later a group of these were refurbished by Bulleid and placed in sets for the 'Bournemouth Limited'. The interior after the work was carried out is shown and the colour scheme was beige.

Below THIRD-CLASS BRAKE CARRIAGE

A compartment in third-class brake no. 3791 which was used for Bournemouth services in 1938.

Above FIRST-CLASS DINING SALOON

The two 'Bournemouth Limited' sets had a first-class dining saloon in the formation and these were also refurbished, being around ten years old. The two carriages were no. 7940 and no. 7943 and the interior of one is shown.

Below COMPOSITE CARRIAGE – NO. 5664

Maunsell composite no. 5664 was included in the 'Bournemouth Limited' set. The coach had been built in 1932 for service on ex-LSWR routes.

FIRST
7750 E

Above CINEMA COACH – NO. 1308S
Composite carriage no. 5537 was destroyed by a fire in 1938, yet the underframe was salvaged. This became the basis of a cinema coach ordered soon after. Whilst the London & North Eastern Railway converted two carriages in the mid-1930s which showed moving pictures when travelling on the East Coast Main Line, the SR vehicle fulfilled a different role by playing instructional films related to the Second World War at places across the company's system. There was seating for 60 people on 15 bench seats. The projection room was served by a generator van, no. 1309S, built at the same time. The set survived the war and many years into the post-Nationalisation period. This image dates from c. 1940.

Opposite above SECOND-CLASS SALOON
As mentioned, the SR built some unclassified saloons that could be used to suit different services, though still being of a high standard. In 1938, both older saloons and newer brake saloons were permanently classified seconds, mainly for employment on boat trains. Numbered 4391-4397, the interior of one of the vehicles is shown.

Opposite below FIRST-CLASS BRAKE CARRIAGE – NO. 7750
First-class brake carriage no. 7750 was built for the continental boat trains just after Grouping. There were four compartments and small saloon. Of the group constructed to diagram 552, two were refurbished in 1938 and no. 7750's interior has been captured following the process.

Above COMPOSITE CARRIAGE – NO. 5751
As the war halted new carriage construction, Bulleid had plenty of time to develop new designs. The first composite carriage to embody these was no. 5751 and the interior of a first-class compartment is shown in 1945.

Below BULLEID BOURNEMOUTH SET – NO. 290
Ten sets of six carriages were introduced by Bulleid for the Bournemouth route from August 1947 to March 1948. No. 290 was the first in traffic.

Above COMPOSITE CARRIAGE – NO. 5726

For West of England expresses, 18 three-carriage sets were formed in 1945-1946. The formation was a brake third, composite and brake third. No. 5726 was a seven-compartment first/third composite and joined set no. 980.

Below THIRD-CLASS OPEN SALOON

Open saloons for third-class passengers were built in numbers just before and after Nationalisation. Completed to diagram 2017, the interior of one of these vehicles is below.

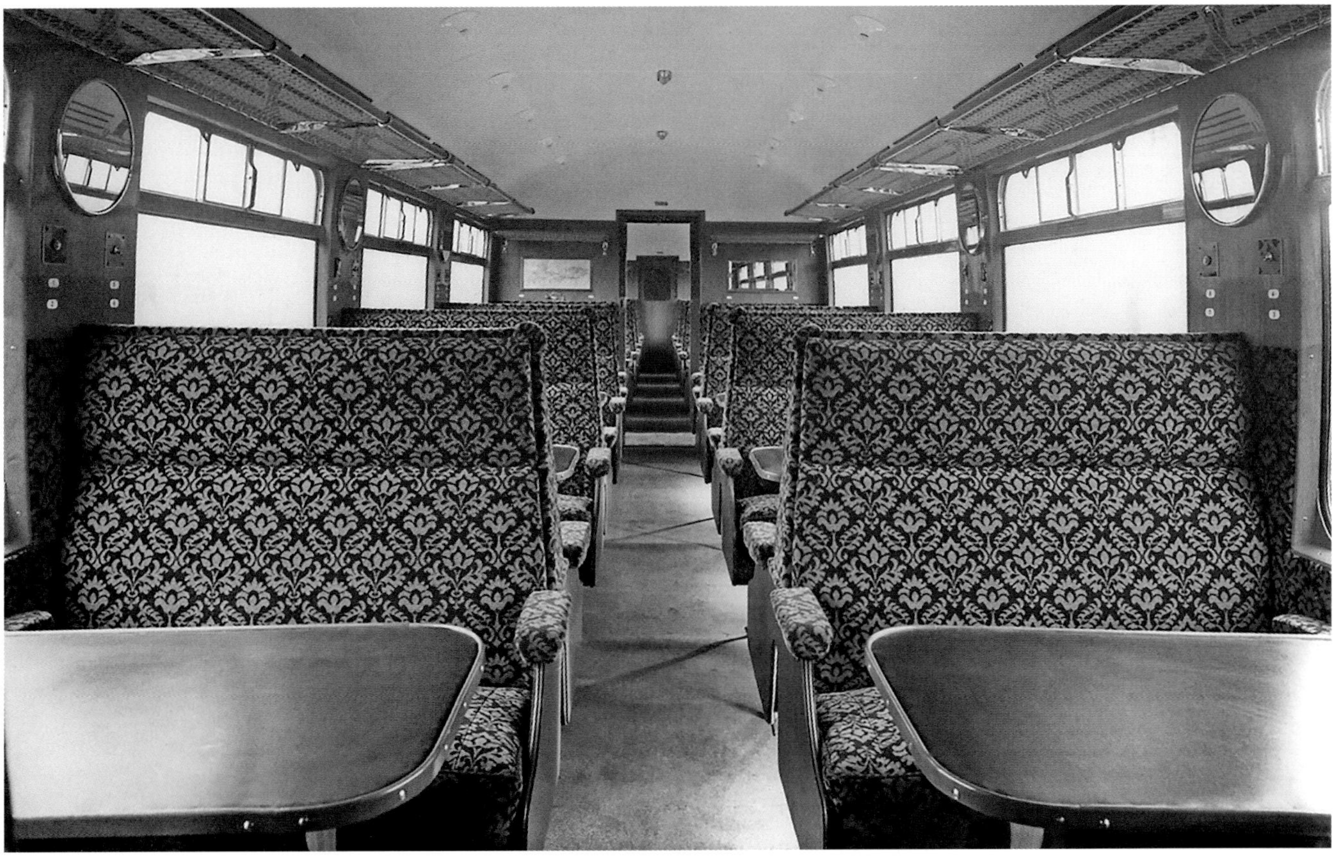

Above EASTLEIGH CARRIAGE WORKS
The area north of Southampton was quiet and rural when the London & Southampton Railway, later LSWR, arrived in 1839. The line cut through the area between the settlements of Eastleigh and Bishopstoke and within the next two decades was also the site of two major junctions for the route to Gosport, as well as Salisbury. The area's importance further increased before the end of the 19th century as the LSWR chose the Bishopstoke side of the main line for the construction of new workshops. The company's site at Nine Elms, which had become too small once before during the mid-1860s, had again reached capacity. Though several other locations were considered, Bishopstoke had the most scope for development and in 1891 the site, known as Eastleigh, was ready for carriage and wagon construction. Covering 46 acres, the shops had a floor area of 456,000 sq. ft and all facilities necessary for construction from raw materials to finished product. When first opened, 1,150 were employed there. Under the SR, the shops were reorganised, as new wagon construction was centralised at Ashford Works. Also, the 'assembly line' method was adopted and in the 1930s a gang of around 30 men was employed on each stage of construction. A coach was said to be capable of being erected in just 21 hours, whilst repairs lasted approx. 14 hours. In the late 1930s, the works began using steel-bodied carriages and transitioned fully after the Second World War. The image above shows construction taking place at Eastleigh before Nationalisation.

Opposite above ALLHALLOWS-ON-SEA STATION
The Hundred of Hoo Railway connected Gravesend and Port Victoria in the late 19th century as the South Eastern Railway hoped to turn the latter into a major port. However, this did not materialise and the Southern Railway promoted a holiday resort to the north at Allhallows-on-Sea. A station opened there on a new branch during May 1932. A Wainwright H Class 0-4-4T is with a train here.

Opposite below BASINGSTOKE STATION
Ready for traffic in June 1839, Basingstoke station was a terminus for around a year as the London & South Western Railway progressed towards Southampton. During 1848, the Great Western Railway established a broad gauge station nearby, then later moved to a site adjacent allowing a connection. The GWR facility closed in 1932 and was subsequently cleared.

RAILWAY STATIONS

Above CATERHAM STATION
The independent Caterham Railway opened in August 1856 and was later bought by the SER. The latter rebuilt the line in the late 1890s and early 1900s, with a new station provided at Caterham. Electrification was carried out in 1928 and an EMU service is at the platform here.

Opposite above BRADING STATION
The Isle of Wight Railway built Brading station on the Ryde to Shanklin route during 1864. An extension to Ventnor followed soon after, whilst a branch from Brading to Bembridge opened in 1882.

Opposite below BUDE STATION
Local residents pressured the LSWR to extend a branch from Okehampton to Bude in the late 19th century. Though initially authorised and completed as far as Holsworthy, the company declined to finish the route and nearly 20 years elapsed before the remainder opened to traffic.

Above CHESSINGTON SOUTH STATION

Conceived as a main line relief, the Chessington branch only reached Chessington South station (opened in May 1939) before the war stopped the project. A horse bus to the nearby Chessington Zoo is outside, c. 1945.

Below CORFE CASTLE STATION

Open between 1885 and 1972, Corfe Castle station has subsequently become part of the Swanage heritage railway. The signal box was lost in the 1950s but has since been restored.

Above DUNGENESS STATION

A line from Ashford to Rye and Hastings opened in 1851. This skirted the western edge of Romney Marsh and subsequent developments saw lines built eastwards. The Lydd Railway was authorised to make a junction with the main line at Appledore with a route from Dungeness. Whilst Lydd was an established settlement, there was little at Dungeness apart from the lighthouse. This stands in the background from the basic station, open between 1883 and 1937, in this image. The lighthouse dated from the early 20th century and replaced Wyatt's Tower, the base of which survives in the background.

Below CLOCK HOUSE STATION

Clock House station opened on the Mid-Kent line during May 1890 as the London suburbs grew. Electrified in 1926, the facility is still open for passengers to London Charing Cross or Hayes.

Above ELMSTEAD WOODS STATION

A later addition to the main line following quadrupling, Elmstead Woods station opened 1904 as Elmstead. Four years later, the name changed and this has remained in use to present.

Below EASTBOURNE STATION

In the early 20th century, the London & North Western Railway and LB&SCR agreed to co-operate with a service from Liverpool to Brighton and Eastbourne. Named the 'Sunny South Express', the train is at Eastbourne with B2 Class no. 323 *William Cubitt*.

Above GRAVESEND WEST STREET STATION
Gravesend West Street station was the second in the town, opening as Gravesend during May 1886. Built by the LC&DR, following amalgamation with the SER, the name changed to Gravesend West Street and from 1949 to closure in 1953, the title was Gravesend West. The site was later cleared.

Below FAYGATE STATION
Faygate station is on the first stage of the Mid-Sussex route which opened in February 1848.

FOREST HILL
WAREHOUSING
Rinso
CAMP
COFFEE
EMU

BEAWORTHY
SOUTHERN

Above HASTINGS STATION
Hastings station opened in February 1851 as the SER completed a line from Ashford via Rye. This had been instigated by the Brighton, Lewes & Hastings Railway which gave the SER construction rights, though later joined in with the formation of the LB&SCR. The BL&HR had started the section from Brighton to Lewes before amalgamation and the LB&SCR continued to progress eastwards, with the SER opening the final connection during 1851. Another year passed before the SER's Tonbridge to Hastings line was ready for operations. As two companies ran to Hastings, the station had separate booking offices and platforms. After Grouping, this was unnecessary and the SR rebuilt Hastings station in 1931. The image above was taken following reconstruction.

Opposite above FOREST HILL STATION
The London & Croydon Railway developed from the Surrey Iron Railway which was an early plateway from Wandsworth to Croydon. The success of early railway undertakings using locomotives inspired the SIR to switch and the L&CR was authorised in 1835 to connect with the London & Greenwich Railway at Bermondsey. The construction project lasted four years and was around triple the estimated cost of £180,000. Six stations were on the route from London Bridge to Croydon, with one being Dartmouth Arms which six years later became Forest Hill station. In the early 1840s, the London & Brighton Railway joined the L&CR as did the South Eastern Railway. The L&BR and L&CR merged in 1846 to create the London, Brighton & South Coast Railway. Forest Hill station saw some modifications during the 1850s and 1860s, also surviving damage from bombs in the Second World War. The buildings, including a clock tower, were cleared in the 1970s and replaced by modern facilities.

Opposite below HALWILL STATION
Several stations were on the Bude branch from Meldon Junction on the line to Plymouth. One was Halwill, which was named Beaworthy when opened on 20th January 1879. The North Cornwall Railway started their route to Padstow from the station in 1886 and completed construction in stages up to 1899. Following the end of the first stage to Launceston, Beaworthy station became Halwill Junction and this title lasted to Grouping when shortened to Halwill. The NCR was supported and worked by the LSWR, with the latter absorbing the NCR subsequently. This view of Halwill is from c. 1930.

Above LITTLEHAMPTON STATION
Arundel & Littlehampton station opened on the Portsmouth to Brighton line during 1846. This was a distance from the town and in the early 1860s a branch was built. Before the end of the 19th century, the junction for the branch was rationalised to improve traffic flow. The line was electrified in 1938 and the original station buildings replaced during the 1980s.

Below LYME REGIS STATION
Struggling for financial backing, the Axminster & Lyme Regis Railway took advantage of the Light Railway Act to construct a branch from the main line in the early 20th century.

Above LYMINGE STATION
A line through the Elham Valley was built by the SER between 1884 and 1889. The first section from Folkestone to Barham was ready in 1887 and included Lyminge station.

Below LYMINGTON PIER STATION
At the end of the Lymington branch was Lymington Pier station which was built five years after the original route. Opening on 1st May 1884, the station remains in use.

Above LYNTON & LYNMOUTH STATION

The Lynton & Barnstaple Railway opened using a 1 ft 11½ in. gauge line in 1898. Running for 19 miles, the route went from Barnstaple north eastwards to Lynton & Lynmouth station. Seen c. 1930, the station closed with the line in 1935.

Below MARGATE STATION

The SR received the competing lines of the SER and LC&DR around Ramsgate and Margate at Grouping. In the mid-1920s, the SR sought to rationalise arrangements and improve connections. Stations were closed and replaced, including Margate which opened in 1926 to the design of SR architect E.M. Fry. Pictured around that time, the station has been listed subsequently.

Above ORPINGTON STATION
To reduce the length of the original route from London to Folkestone, the SER built a new line from Chislehurst to Tonbridge during the late 1860s. Orpington was a station on the route and opened on 8th March 1868. In the early 20th century, reconstruction was carried out as new platforms were installed and the line was electrified between 1925 and 1935.

Below PADSTOW STATION
Adams O2 Class 0-4-4T no. 182 has a train at Padstow station, c. 1930.

Above PETTS WOOD STATION
The growth of Petts Wood as a suburban settlement in the early 1920s saw the establishment of a station during July 1928 which was done at the expense of the developer.

Below RAMSGATE TOWN STATION
In the mid-1840s, the SER branched from Ashford to Canterbury, Ramsgate and Margate. Ramsgate Town station, opened as Ramsgate during 1846, was a terminus which meant services onward to Margate had to reverse. After Grouping, the SR revised the network in the area and closed both stations in Ramsgate, building two new facilities. Ramsgate Town shut in 1926 and is pictured c. 1923.

Above **ROTHERFIELD & MARK CROSS STATION**

The line from Eastbourne to Tunbridge Wells was built in stages between 1849 and 1880. Rotherfield & Mark Cross station was on the last section and opened to traffic in September 1880. The facility replaced Rotherfield on the line to Lewes and this became Crowborough. Rotherfield & Mark Cross closed in 1965 and the buildings are now private residences.

Below **SITTINGBOURNE STATION**

Sittingbourne opened on 25th January 1858, with just station building and platforms provided. In 1863, a roof spanning the platforms was erected and this lasted through to the early 1950s. The SR installed new goods sidings following Grouping.

Above ST DENYS STATION

North of Southampton, a station opened as Portswood in 1861. Five years later, the facility moved south as a branch to Portsmouth was built. The new station was named St Denys and continues to serve the district. Adams F6 Class 0-4-4T no. 360 is also seen light engine.

Above SUTTON STATION
Following the formation of the LB&SCR, the company opened a line from West Croydon to Epsom. One of the intermediate stations was Sutton, 14 miles from central London. Under the SR, the station was rebuilt in the late 1920s and the new facility is pictured above.

Opposite below SUNNINGDALE STATION
The Staines, Wokingham & Woking Junction Railway completed a line from Staines to Wokingham in mid-1856 which the LSWR used to access Reading. Running powers were given by the SER for the short remaining distance from Wokingham. Sunningdale station was on the route from opening.

Below TATTENHAM CORNER STATION
In the late 19th century, a branch was built from Purley to Tattenham Corner. The station at the latter was opened on 4th June 1901 and at this time, the SER had taken over operations. From the First World War to 1928, the station was closed to the public, though used for race specials, and reopened when electrification was carried out in the late 1920s. The station's signage advertises this fact in this image from c. 1935.

Above VICTORIA STATION

With many places of importance in London north of the River Thames, the railway companies operating to Southern England had to improve connections to them for passengers. During the late 1850s, several companies joined a scheme to extend across the river and establish a new station at Victoria Street. The LB&SCR and LC&DR were the main companies involved, with the Great Western and London & North Western Railways also having investment in the project. Construction was carried out relatively quickly and the first trains ran to the LB&SCR's portion of the facility in October 1860. The LC&DR's section took a little longer and was ready in late August 1862. As with other stations, when traffic increased later in the 19th century, improvements were necessary. The LB&SCR rebuilt their station at the turn of the century and the new facility opened in 1908. The Grosvenor Hotel was also largely remodelled during this period. Whilst the two sides of the station were largely independent, after the formation of the SR modifications saw greater integration of the two portions. Electrification of the lines was also carried out. The frontage of the ex-LB&SCR side of Victoria station is seen here, c. 1930.

Opposite above WALMER STATION

As part of the branch from Ashford to Canterbury, Ramsgate and Margate, the SER laid a line from Minster which ran southward to Sandwich and Deal. Terminating at the latter, there were proposals for extensions to meet the main line at Dover but these failed to progress for a number of years. The SER ultimately entered into a partnership with the rival LC&DR to build the Deal & Dover Joint Line which was completed in 1881. One of two stations opened was Walmer which also served the nearby village of Kingsdown.

Opposite below WATERINGBURY STATION

A branch from the Dover line was built by the SER in the mid-1840s. This left the route at Paddock Wood and headed northwards to Maidstone. Wateringbury station was amongst the stations opened at the time and continues to operate, being granted Grade II listed status during the mid-1980s. The branch was later extended from Maidstone to Strood.

WALMER
FOR
KINGSDOWN

WATERINGBURY

WATERLOO STATION
SOUTHERN RAILWA

WARTIME

Above **BRIGHTON WORKS**

After Grouping, the SR reorganised the workshops to deal with specific areas. Eastleigh mainly handled locomotives, Ashford the wagon stock and carriages were dealt with at Lancing. Brighton Works was a casualty of the changes as many of the tasks were redistributed elsewhere in 1928 and the shops were retained for running repairs, as well as EMU maintenance. By the late 1930s, just 3½ acres of the 7 acres of workshop space available were in use and the employees numbered just 253 men. At the outbreak of war, a major effort was made to re-equip Brighton Works and heavy machinery was sent from a number of locations whilst the workforce swelled to 755 men and 214 women employed full time. There were several Government contracts awarded to Brighton, including tank and gun components. The works also returned to locomotive construction as orders were placed for Bulleid Q1 Class 0-6-0s and 'Battle of Britain' and 'West Country' Pacifics. Sir William Stanier's 8F Class 2-8-0 design produced for the London Midland & Scottish Railway was chosen to be standard for the War Department which needed them for service in conflict zones. The Railway Executive Committee, which oversaw the 'Big Four' during the Second World War, also ordered a large number for use across the country to help the war effort. As part of this, Brighton erected 68 8Fs in 1943 and 1944. The London & North Eastern Railway also purchased 68 8Fs to help with movement of war materials and 25 of these were produced at Brighton. A number of 8Fs are being erected at Brighton in the image above.

Opposite **WATERLOO STATION**

As with Victoria station, Waterloo was the result of the L&SWR wanting better connections to Central London. The original terminus at Nine Elms was a distance short of this and an extension to Waterloo Bridge was authorised in the mid-1840s, opening towards the end of the decade. Waterloo station was to be just a stepping stone on the path to a terminus on the north bank of the Thames, yet this failed to come to fruition and the facilities were fully upgraded at the turn of the century. The work took some time to complete and finally ceased for opening in 1922, accommodating 21 platforms. The main entrance was designed by James Rob Scott who created a memorial to company employees killed in the First World War. The Roman goddesses of war and peace were sculpted by Charles Whiffen. Under the SR, Waterloo saw signalling and track improvements, as well as several electrification schemes.

HAVANT STATION

Soldiers load stores into an SR goods van at Havant station on 15th July 1942.

Above WOMEN WAR WORKERS
By 1944, around 10,000 women were employed as part of the SR's workforce. They took many roles and a quartet are variously engaged at a station.

Below TROOP SPECIAL
Operation Dynamo saw nearly 350,000 men evacuated from Dunkirk to ports along the South Coast. A large number of trains were necessary to disperse the soldiers and one is seen carrying allied troops here.

BIBLIOGRAPHY

Allen, Cecil J. *Titled Trains of Great Britain*. 1983.
Bradley, D.L. *Locomotives of the L.B.&S.C.R.: Part 1*. 1969.
Bradley, D.L. *Locomotives of the L.B.&S.C.R.: Part 2*. 1972.
Bradley, D.L. *Locomotives of the L.B.&S.C.R.: Part 3*. 1974.
Bradley, D.L. *Locomotives of the Southern Railway: Part 1*. 1975.
Bradley, D.L. *Locomotives of the Southern Railway: Part 2*. 1976.
Bradley, D.L. *The Locomotive History of the London, Chatham & Dover Railway*. 1979.
Bradley, D.L. *The Locomotives of the South Eastern Railway*. 1963.
Bradley, D.L. *The Locomotives of the South Eastern & Chatham Railway*. 1961.
Cooper, B.K. *Southern Railway Handbook*. 1983.
Darwin, Bernard. *War on the Line: The Southern Railway in War-Time*. 1946.
Hawkins, Chris and George Reeve. *An Historical Survey of Southern Sheds*. 2001.
King, Mike. *An Illustrated History of Southern Coaches*. 2003.
Marsden, Colin J. *Southern Electric Multiple-Units: 1898-1948*. 1983.
Quick, Michael. *Railway Passenger Stations in Great Britain: A Chronology*. 2009.
Rayner, Brian (Ed.). *Southern Electrics: A Pictorial Survey*. 1975.
Swift, Peter. *Locomotives in Detail: Six – Maunsell 4-4-0 Schools Class*. 2006.
Townroe, S.C. *'Arthurs', 'Nelsons' & 'Schools' at Work*. 1983.
Winkworth, D.W. *Southern Titled Trains*. 1988.
Wragg, David. *The Southern Railway Handbook: 1923-1947*. 2003.
